Stepping Stones to Success

A Two Year Quality Circle Time Programme For Early Years

Helen Sonnet & Pat Child

Foreword by Jenny Mosley

Positive Press

Published by:
Positive Press Ltd
28A Gloucester Road
Trowbridge
Wiltshire BA14 OAA

First Published © 2002 Positive Press Ltd
Re-Printed © 2004
Text copyright © Helen Sonnet & Pat Child
Illustrations by Mark Cripps

ISBN 0-9540585-0-X

Printed by:

HERON PRESS
19-24 White Hays North
West Wilts Trading Estate
Westbury
Wiltshire BA13 4JT

Warm thanks to:

1.

The practitioners in Guernsey who have embraced Quality Circle Time with enthusiasm. They have given willingly of their time and expertise to refine the lesson plans.

The children of Guernsey who have been a joy to work with. Their contributions and enjoyment of the lessons provided the inspiration for this book.

Marian Dowling, early years specialist and former HMI, for finding the time to read and review the book so positively.

Finally, thanks must go to Jenny Mosley for without her vision and support this book would not have been written.

Foreword

The curriculum guidance for the foundation stage (QCA) formalised the recognition that children's early years are a vital stage in their educational development that needs to be properly catered for.

The Quality Circle Time model, used now in hundreds of schools in the U.K. is equally 'powerful' for this age range. It offers a positive holistic approach to meeting the emotional needs of children. It promotes the development of self-esteem, giving children the confidence to learn, and respect and empathy for others, so vital in forming good relationships

This book by Helen Sonnet and Pat Child is an invaluable addition to the current Quality Circle Time resources. It sets out a carefully planned and structured programme of P.S.E. sessions that will give the practitioner confidence to take the children through the two years of the foundation stage.

Helen Sonnet, a former primary school teacher, has been involved with the Quality Circle Time model for 12 years. She has gently watched its development, helped with other previous publications and is co-author with me of the book 'Here We Go Round,' a seminal book for the foundation stage. She therefore understands the essence of the model.

Pat Child has been an enthusiast of Quality Circle Time since attending the accredited 'Train the Trainers' course. At that time Pat was the headteacher of a large infant school and was committed to using the model in her school. Subsequently, she became the PSHE co-ordinator for Guernsey and is now involved in training early years practitioners. Pat encourages practitioners to make PSE development an integral aspect of all activities, but she also advises the use of Quality Circle Time as part of a planned approach for delivering the PSE programme. Guernsey teachers value the written lesson plans and are enthusiastically using them in their own settings.

I truly believe that all practitioners will find this book a really useful and valuable resource to support the personal, social and emotional development of all children.

Jenny Mosley.

Introduction

The Quality Circle Time book, 'Here We Go Round', written by Jenny Mosley and Helen Sonnet was published in March 2001 as a direct response to recent developments in early years education and specifically the publication in May 2000 by the Qualifications and Curriculum Authority (QCA) of the booklet 'Curriculum Guidance for The Foundation Stage'.

It has been recognised how critical these early years are to children's development and, for the first time, this age bracket, (from 3 – 5 years), has been given a distinct identity. The objective of the guidance was to help practitioners provide a high quality integrated, early education, enabling children to develop key learning and social skills and thereby have the necessary foundations for entering school. It aim is to provide all children with the opportunity to 'experience the very best start to their education' and to 'help practitioners provide learning and teaching experiences of the highest quality'.

Six areas of learning are defined for the foundation stage, outlining the early learning goals for each area. These goals 'establish expectations for most children to reach by the end of the foundation stage'. 'Stepping stones' that show 'the developing knowledge, skills, understanding and attitudes that children need if they are to achieve these early learning goals', are used in the guidance to help practitioners plan an appropriate curriculum.

This book, a sequel to 'Here We Go Round', focuses in depth on one area of learning; Personal, Social and Emotional Development. Using a combination of familiar, well loved circle games and new ideas, it provides a unique two year programme of Quality Circle Time activities for the relevant stepping stones and early learning goals. Although these activities relate directly to the stepping stones and early learning goals in the Curriculum guidance, they are equally relevant to requirements of the Scottish, Welsh and Northern Irish Early Years Guidelines.

All the activities included in this book have been tried successfully in nursery settings and reception classes. A selection of written responses from practitioners and teachers collated during the book's 'trialling period' testify to the support it can offer:

"Brilliant, really helps me to fulfil the learning objectives of the foundation stage."

"Gave me lots of ideas that the children love."

"Children love talking to and about the puppets."

"The activities definitely encourage the children to sit and really listen."

"All my group enjoy taking part and often ask if it is time for Circle Time."

"The plans are clear and save us a lot of time in planning."

"It provides a time when we can observe and assess the children against the stepping stone objectives."

"We learn so much about our children in the Circle Time sessions."

Personal, social and emotional development

Personal, social and emotional development is about 'emotional wellbeing, knowing who you are and where you fit in and feeling good about yourself. It is also about developing respect for others, social competence and a positive disposition to learn.' (QCA).

Personal, social and emotional development is vital for success in all areas of learning. Children need to be equipped with the requisite learning and social skills so they can then have the confidence to know what is required of them and how to accomplish this.

The early learning goals for this area are:

For dispositions and attitudes:

♦ Continue to be interested, excited and motivated to learn.

♦ Be confident to try new activities, initiate ideas and speak in a familiar group.

♦ Maintain attention, concentrate and sit quietly when appropriate.

For self–confidence and self–esteem:

♦ Respond to significant experiences, showing a range of feelings when appropriate.

♦ Have a developing awareness of their own needs, views and feelings and be sensitive to the needs, views and feelings of others.

♦ Have a developing respect for their own cultures and beliefs and those of other people.

For making relationships:

♦ Form good relationships with adults and peers.

♦ Work as part of a group or class, taking turns and sharing fairly, understanding the need for agreed values and codes of behaviour for groups of people, including adults and children, to work together harmoniously.

For behaviour and self-control:

♦ Understand what is right, what is wrong, and why.

♦ Consider the consequences of their words and actions for themselves and others.

For self-care:

♦ Dress and undress independently and manage their own personal hygiene.

♦ Select and use activities and resources independently.

For a sense of community:

♦ Understand that people have different needs, cultures and beliefs, that need to be treated with respect.

♦ Understand that they can expect others to treat their needs, views, cultures and beliefs with respect.

Practitioners and teachers are required to ' plan a curriculum that helps children make good progress towards and where appropriate, beyond these goals', (QCA).

Stepping stones

The curriculum guidance identifies 'stepping stones' that show the common pattern of progress that children make towards the early learning goals. These stepping stones identify the knowledge, skills, understanding and attitudes the children will need to reach those goals. They do not constitute a curriculum themselves, but provide a framework around which practitioners can plan activities for the children which help them make connections.

Stepping stones may relate to one aspect of an early learning goal, to aspects of more than one early learning goal or closely linked goals within an area of learning. Every aspect of learning for young children is interelated, therefore most stepping stones within one area of learning have links with other areas. Individual stepping stones may focus on just one aspect of an area of learning such as a skill, or knowledge or attitude.

Whilst the stepping stones are not age–related, they can indicate which learning goals the children might be unable to reach by the end of the foundation stage, and help practitioners to create individual learning plans. Some children may attain confidence in later stepping stones, but not in all of the earlier ones and the rate of progress through the stepping stones will vary from child to child.

Putting the guidelines into practice

Children arrive at their pre–school settings from a variety of backgrounds with differing moral and cultural values. Some will be outgoing, confident, have high self–esteem, be independent, ready to integrate and take on new ideas and challenges. Other children may be shy, withdrawn, unwilling to take part in activities, integrate with the other children, or need constant adult support. The children will have different experiences of nurturing, displays of affection, social occasions and opportunities for interaction with others. In other words, all children will be unique, have varying needs and be at different stages of development.

Children in the foundation stage are active both mentally and physically. They need to be presented with a huge variety of experiences so that they can express themselves in as many ways as possible. They are beginning to solve problems and to be able to hypothesise and reason. They need to feel safe enough to make mistakes. They need opportunities to interact with others in a conducive environment where they feel valued and confident.

Good early years' provision must take into account all of these factors. Quality Circle Time, with its democratic framework and carefully planned strategies, can meet these criteria.

The Quality Circle Time Model

The Quality Circle Time model, devised by Jenny Mosley, is now used in hundreds of settings and schools throughout the United Kingdom. The model has received considerable acclaim and its success is recognised in many OFSTED reports. The following comments relate to recent reports for nursery and infant schools.

The weekly Circle Time for each class enables pupils of all ages, at their own level, to reflect on aspects of their lives, to discuss moral and social issues and to express with confidence their understanding of right and wrong and their sense of justice. Pupils learn to listen to others, to be tolerant of other viewpoints and to respect fellow pupils.

The good relationships within the school and the successful Circle Times have raised pupils' self–esteem and they know and understand what is expected of them.

Staff generally make clear their expectations for good behaviour and children respond to their encouragement and praise at 'Circle Time', when children are encouraged to listen carefully to instructions and the stories and rhymes. Children are learning to recognise right from wrong and are kind and respectful to each other, especially the younger children and those from other cultures and beliefs. Children show confidence and self–respect, especially in the friendly way they introduce themselves, talk to visitors and tell their 'news' during Circle Time.

The guidelines for running Quality Circle Time ensure that it provides a safe environment in which all children feel equally valued. Once it has been established, Quality Circle Time offers an effective forum in which to promote respect, trust, empathy and understanding. It is also a valuable behaviour management strategy as the children are encouraged to become self–regulating within the circle. Responsibility for good behaviour is shared by everyone. For younger children, practising social skills through planned interaction with others helps develop sociability.

In order to create an effective learning culture, Quality Circle Time needs to be conducted according to the guidelines laid down in this book and, if possible, after training from an accredited consultant, (see Resources Section for training opportunities).

Quality Circle Time should not merely be :

- ◆ playing games for their own sake

- ◆ a 'show-and-tell' circle

- ◆ an unplanned chat time

- ◆ a quick fix for difficult behaviour – it is a continual process of plan, do and review

- ◆ being nice to one another on cue

- ◆ a way of filling in spare time, it should be time-tabled.

The success of this model depends on the emphasis on 'quality'.

For this reason it is important to evaluate your circle sessions regularly to ensure that they are fulfilling the role intended for them.

How Quality Circle Time upholds the principles for early years education

♦ Quality Circle Time can ensure that all children feel included, secure and valued.

♦ Quality Circle Time can build on children's existing knowledge and experience. It is motivational and promotes a positive disposition to learn.

♦ Quality Circle Time's carefully structured activities aim to prevent failure.

♦ Quality Circle Time includes all children regardless of ethnicity, culture, religion, language, background, additional needs, disability, gender or ability.

♦ Quality Circle Time informs and involves parents.

♦ Quality Circle Time activities are planned to provide for differences in children's starting points and variety of their needs.

♦ Quality Circle Time provides opportunities for teaching and learning.

♦ Quality Circle Time helps practitioners observe and respond appropriately to children.

♦ Quality Circle Time provides well planned, purposeful activity.

♦ Quality Circle Time allows children to explore, experiment, plan and make decisions for themselves.

Quality Circle Time and personal, social and emotional development.

Quality Circle Time is especially well suited to personal, social and emotional development. Its structure and strategies benefit both children and adults.

Quality Circle Time helps children to:

- feel safe in a secure environment and develop trust in their group

- have the opportunity to learn from others

- learn about friendship and relationships

- develop a positive disposition to learn

- have opportunities for problem-solving

- have opportunities for initiating activities

- develop key language and social skills

- express their feelings in an appropriate way

- form positive relationships with adults and other children

- express choices, plan and make decisions

- take turns, share and co-operate

- try new activities

- understand and use agreed codes of behaviour

- consider their own and other peoples' needs

- consider moral values and understand what is right and what is wrong

- show an appropriate range of feelings

Quality Circle Time helps practitioners to:

♦ develop good relationships between adults, children and children and adults

♦ give positive encouragement

♦ provide positive role models

♦ plan activities with a relevant focus

♦ provide a motivating environment

♦ provide positive images of gender, race, religion and additional needs

♦ provide activities that acknowledge the diversity of religious beliefs and cultural backgrounds

♦ help children develop independence

♦ provide emotional support for vulnerable children

♦ provide new ideas and challenges

♦ promote the notion of equality

♦ initiate collective responsibility for the promotion of self-esteem and positive behaviour

♦ establish a forum where children can help one another

♦ develop role play in a safe environment

♦ develop group cohesion and positive group dynamics

♦ develop the key learning skills of listening and speaking

Quality Circle Time and emotional intelligence

For many years, education was mainly concerned with IQ and academic achievement, but the notion of 'other intelligences' has gained ground in recent years. Research carried out by Howard Gardner (1993) expounded the theory of multiple intelligences and Daniel Goleman (1996) added weight to this theory with his book 'Emotional Intelligence', outlining five main areas. These are:

- ◆ Knowing one's emotions
- ◆ Managing one's emotions
- ◆ Motivating oneself
- ◆ Recognising emotions in others
- ◆ Handling relationships

Moreover, Goleman states that children have 'windows of opportunity' when they are receptive to 'emotional coaching'. This idea is supported by current research carried out by neuroscientists such as Professor Colin Blakemore, who argue that the brain is set up during the early years of childhood to learn important social and relationship skills. Recent scientific evidence also suggests that such learning may only be really successful at this stage of development because practising these important social skills may actually alter the growing brain. Professor Blakemore considers that, as the requisite skills are not always taught in the home, the education system should focus on these rather than academic skills during the foundation stage. Quality Circle Time can play a valuable role in helping children achieve these important qualities. As Jenny Mosley explains in her book 'More Quality Circle Time' (1998),

> *Circle Time provides the ideal opportunity for all our intelligences to be stretched and challenged. Children are not only specifically taught the skills they need for personal and social development, but they also learn self–awareness and how to recognise and monitor their own feelings. In addition they are taught strategies to handle their and others' feelings in a respectful and sensitive way.*

They become self-motivated through an understanding of the benefits and freedom that develop from being able to regulate their own responses and take charge of their own destinies. Circle Time places great emphasis on the need for empathy, for understanding another's world, and helps the children to explore and discover successful ways of interacting with others.

References

Gardner, H. (1993) *Multiple Intelligence - The Theory in Practice*. London, Basic Books.

Goleman, D. (1996) *Emotional Intelligence*. London, Bloomsbury

Blakemore, Professor C. (2001) cited in *Brian Waves* by Wallace, W. *Nursery World*. Page 10.

Golden Rules

The Quality Circle Time model advocates the use of Golden Rules which should be prominently displayed in every room of the preschool setting or reception area. These are the moral values that will inform and develop the culture of the group. Displaying the rules makes it easier to establish uniformity, ensuring that all practitioners use the same language and emphasise the same values. The Golden Rules used by the Quality Circle Time model in infant and primary schools are:

Do be gentle, don't hurt anybody.

Do be kind and helpful, don't hurt people's feelings.

Do be honest, don't cover up the truth.

Do work hard, don't waste time.

Do look after property, don't waste or damage things.

Do listen to people, don't interrupt.

These will be too complex for very young children and it may be better to just start with two positive statements i.e.

Do be gentle.

Do be kind and helpful.

Generally speaking, the other Golden Rules are gradually introduced from the second term of reception onwards. A further Golden Rule that is useful with young children is:

Do play well, don't spoil others' games.

When you make your displays, do use gold card or paint to symbolically emphasise the 'quality' that these rules will bring to your setting or school life. Some practitioners like to make a wall display from photographs of the children modelling good behaviour with an appropriate text underneath e.g Sasha and Joe tidying up, Lola and Aneena playing well together. You can then draw the children's attention to desired behaviour with a visual example.

An OFSTED Report for an infant school cited the very good provision made for pupils' moral development with a clear code of behaviour based on the Golden Rules. These were clearly understood and respected by the pupils, who knew right from wrong and recognised acceptable and unacceptable behaviour.

Golden Time

Golden Time is another feature of the Quality Circle Time model and provides a successful whole class incentive. This is a privilege for keeping the Golden Rules and is a very effective way of promoting positive behaviour once you are sure the children know right from wrong.

Golden Time could be a short daily or longer weekly celebration of the children's ability to keep the Golden Rules. It is a choosing time with special games and activities, which are just used for these occasions. Alternatively, it can be used for a special group activity. The value of Golden Time, as long as it remains a *quality* time for the children, is that it can be used very effectively as a sanctions system, i.e. loss of Golden Time. For young children this system involves three stages.

First stage

A large yellow sun is constructed from thick card. The sun should have a happy, smiling face. Yellow clothes pegs are used for the rays of the sun and on each peg, print the name of a child, and if available, attach a photograph of the child's face. The reverse side of each peg is painted grey. The sun represents Golden Time and the 'rays' show all the children who are going to enjoy that privilege.

Second stage

A second card construction is made of a sun, partly obscured by a grey cloud. The expression on the sun is less happy. If a child breaks a Golden Rule, they are given a verbal warning. If they fail to respond to the warning, their peg is removed from the sun and placed on the sun and cloud display. This is an interim measure and the peg can be reinstated on the yellow sun if the child heeds the warning.

Third stage

If the child continues to disregard the warning, the peg is placed grey side uppermost onto a third construction, a grey cloud with a sad face. This indicates that the child has lost five minutes of Golden Time. Additional grey pegs can be used to show further loss of time, however it is not a good idea to remove all the privilege. Children should also be given the opportunity to 'earn back' lost Golden Time through behaviour targets, e.g., every half day they reach their target, they can earn back 1 – 5 minutes of Golden Time.

At the beginning of Golden Time, any child with a grey peg must sit apart from the other children with a timer that is set for their 'time out'. Once this has been completed they may join in the activities. Golden Time has been introduced to preschool and reception classes with considerable success, but you need to evaluate whether your children are ready for it. It is important to ensure that Golden Time remains a strong incentive and special for the children. Stourfield First School even created a Golden Room for this quality time:

> *We have transformed a room with £500 of new activities of the children's choice, with golden stars, golden material, golden blinds and even golden confetti adorns the carpet. It's brilliant. We have 'Good News' slips which go home, and deducting minutes of Golden Time has made our discipline policy simple, but so much more effective – no Corridor Club – no hours spent in reprimand. The staff love it – the children love it and the parents love it.*

> *I thought we had a reasonably positive atmosphere, but Golden Time has shot status and self- esteem right to the roof beams.*

Mrs C Kirkham, Headteacher.

Quotes from questionnaires sent to parents a term after Golden Rules and Golden Time had been introduced to their children's school

"I think Golden Rules and Golden Time are an excellent way to teach our children the difference between right and wrong, and what is acceptable behaviour. With the reward at the end, they have something to strive for. My daughter enjoys it and frequently reminds myself and my husband of things we are doing wrong."

"Excellent – a good way to reinforce what should be general good behaviour everywhere."

"I think Golden Rules and Golden Time are very effective for teaching children about feelings and use of property which is difficult to instil in young children. It is sensible and gives the children an aim to reach for rewarding good behaviour. Well done!"

"Since attending this school my child has become much happier and more settled it seems at home and school. She is frequently talking about Golden Time and understands that she will be rewarded for hard work and good behaviour, this is obviously reflected at home, and can only be a positive move. We think it is a great idea. Thank you."

"Our Y2 and Reception children have started introducing the Golden Rules at home. They really respond well when I refer to them, it helped to settle a dispute recently too. Thank you."

Setting up Quality Circle Time

You need to select a suitable area in which to hold Circle Time, where you will be undisturbed. Ideally, the area should be carpeted and large enough for the children to join in the activities with ease. When you first introduce Circle Time, younger children may find it difficult to remain in the circle. Marking a symbolic place for them with cushions, carpet squares or chairs will help them remain in situ and keep the circle round, as it is important that it does not have any corners. It is also a good idea to ensure that possible distractions such as boxes of toys, books or games are not within reach of the children during Circle Time. A new or shy child may want to sit on an adult's lap until accustomed to the proceedings. If your children are sitting cross legged on the floor, some practitioners advocate that they place their open hands, palms upwards on their knees. This aids relaxation and discourages the practice of fiddling with shoes, etc.

Time-tabling circle time

Quality Circle Time should be time tabled at least once a week and should last for fifteen to twenty minutes, although with younger children you may want to shorten this to ten minutes and have more frequent sessions. Make sure that you are well prepared with all that you need for the session, so that you don't keep the children waiting once they are seated. It is important that you hold your Circle Time when both you and the children are feeling fresh; if the children are tired they will find it hard to concentrate on the activities. Because of the dynamics of Circle Time, it is vital that you come to the circle with a positive attitude. The children will quickly recognise a negative atmosphere and this will undermine the value of the session. If you are feeling anxious or irritable, practise a short calming ritual and free your mind of negative thoughts so that you can ensure the time is providing the quality intended.

Circle size

Your circle size will depend on the age and ability of your children and the facilities available to you. If you can, keep the group to a maximum of twelve children. Some settings may not have the facilities to accommodate this, and if you only have the use of a single room, don't worry. Circle Time can be just as effective with larger numbers, as long as you use your adult helpers around the circle to keep the activities flowing. Alternatively, hold a Circle Time with one group while another group is engaged in an outdoor activity.

Each circle must have at least one adult helper and they must all follow the same lesson plan and its accompanying script. As the children become familiar with Circle Time procedures and more practised in conducting the activities, you may like to include all adults and children in full class circles, so that you can develop a sense of their wider community.

Using adult helpers

Encourage all adults involved to sit at the same level as the children, either on the floor or on small chairs. Arrange your helpers so that they sit by those children who are most likely to need help or encouragement to join in the activities, e.g., the youngest children, those who find it difficult to sit still and listen, or any child with additional needs or disabilities.

Generally speaking, Quality Circle Time is sufficiently enjoyable and motivational to deter children from leaving the circle. If a young child leaves the circle and is obviously not ready to participate, let an adult occupy the child with another activity. If an older child leaves the circle, have an adult sit with them, providing encouragement and support to stay.

Involving parents

It is a good idea to send a letter home explaining Quality Circle Time to the parents. They are usually very supportive when they understand the principles and guidelines that inform this activity. Invite parents to join in the Circle Time activities. Not only does this give them the opportunity to see Circle Time in practice, but it also provides additional adult support for the group. The children can make their own special invitations or you could detail the Circle Times that you will be having, outlining the topic of each session.

Children with additional needs or disabilities

One of the main principles of Quality Circle Time is that all children should be included and equally valued within the circle. It is therefore important that any child with special or cultural needs, or a disability, is given the necessary support to enable them to participate in Circle Time. If this means one to one support, the adult involved should be fully briefed on the appropriate level of support that is required and the learning outcome that is desired for that child. For a child whose development is delayed, this might involve simplifying an activity in order to make it meaningful. It is no use simply including a child in the circle, if that child is unlikely to gain anything from the activities; you need to find ways to help the child to participate as fully as possible.

The ground rules of Quality Circle Time

Ground rules are laid down for conducting Quality Circle Time to ensure that it is a positive experience for all children. To begin with, it is a good idea to remind children of these before each session. Thereafter an occasional reminder should be sufficient. The ground rules are as follows:

♦ We will all listen to each other. No one is allowed to interrupt when someone is talking. If an adult needs to interrupt for any reason, s/he should say, "*Excuse me for interrupting, —————————-.*"

♦ We all say positive things in the circle. We must not use put downs or make negative comments, including laughing about another's contribution.

♦ We all have a right to speak, but can choose not to if we so wish.

♦ We can say 'pass' in a round if we do not wish to speak, but we can be given a second chance to speak at the end of the round.

♦ We will only speak if we are holding the 'speaking object' during a round or signalling by hands up or by putting thumbs up and in.

Using a speaking object

When doing a 'round', make it flow more smoothly by using a speaking object which is passed from child to child around the circle. It needs to be something small enough to be held easily in one hand, e.g., a painted wooden egg or a small teddy, 'Talking Ted'. Some practitioners use an object that begins with their special 'sound of the week', thereby reinforcing other curriculum areas.

Each child has a turn to speak when they hold the speaking object, but remember a child can elect to pass and hand the object on. If you find that a child always elects to pass, you can try several methods of encouragement. You might ask the child a question, eliciting a response or have an adult sit by the child to inform the circle of the child's whispered contribution. Another way is to use a glove puppet for the child to whisper to. The puppet 'tells' you what the child has said and you relate it to the rest of the group. Puppets can be used very effectively to draw shy children out. Young children are able to suspend disbelief and the cute furry characters can be very real to them, more attractive and welcoming than an adult. Many practitioners have had major breakthroughs and succeeded in encouraging shy children to talk by using a puppet. Remember to give the shy child particular praise for any effort. If, conversely, you have a child who talks too much, you must find a suitable cut off point and thank them for the contribution, gently emphasising the need to move on so that there will be sufficient time for everyone to speak.

If you have a child who just cannot listen to others without interrupting, have an adult sit by them to offer encouragement and make a point of praising good listening skills.

There may be occasions when a child discloses a serious personal issue such as abuse. Make sure that all the adults in your setting are aware of the correct way to handle such revelations. Allow the child to finish speaking and thank them in the usual way. Don't over–react or ask questions within the circle, follow up the information through the correct channels and procedures later.

Promoting positive behaviour through circle time

Quality Circle Time is the ideal forum in which to promote positive behaviour. The most effective way is to use a pro-active approach of modelling and praising good behaviour. Awarding stickers that commend a desired behaviour is a good method as all the children in the circle can see what is being rewarded. Another helpful practice is the use of 'adjacent praise'. This involves praising a child who is behaving well and who is near the child who is not.

During Quality Circle Time, children are given the opportunity to consider and discuss the impact that certain behaviours, both positive and negative, have on other people. One aim of Circle Time is to gradually instil in the children the ability to monitor and regulate their own behaviours with the support of the group and this is an ongoing process throughout their educational lives. Even at an early age, pre–school children can talk about being kind and helpful and think about how antisocial behaviour affects others.

The quality of the well planned activities of Circle Time are generally sufficient to involve young children in the proceedings. The children's enjoyment creates the motivation and disposition to learn, thereby dispelling the need for negative behaviour. The best way to ensure positive behaviour is to provide interest and stimulation for the children. However, if a child is finding it difficult to join in the activities and is disrupting the group there are several ways to deal with this. You can use an adult helper to support the child within the circle, giving encouragement and prompts to keep the child on track.

Using a visual warning works with some children as it is a constant reminder to behave well. This is a circle of card with a happy face on one side and a sad face on the other side. If a child does not heed a verbal warning, the card is placed, sad face uppermost, beside the child. The practitioner explains that everyone is sad because a Golden Rule has been broken. However, if the child stops breaking the rule everyone will be happy again and the card can be turned over to show the happy face. It is important to remove the warning card once the child has responded to it.

The five skills of circle time

It is important to instruct the children in the skills they will need for Circle Time before you begin the sessions. This can be done as a short routine practised before each Circle Time, which the children enjoy. The five skills are:

- Looking

- Listening

- Speaking

- Thinking

- Concentrating

Talk the children through the following routine:

Point to eyes and say, "*In Circle Time we use our looking skills.*"

Point to ears and say, "*In Circle Time we use our listening skills.*"

Point to mouths and say, "*In Circle Time we use our speaking skills.*"

Place hands on sides of head and say, "*In Circle Time we use our thinking skills.*"

Clasp hands and place in laps, look at practitioner and say, "*In Circle Time we use our concentrating skills.*"

Once the children have learnt this short routine you can say the words while the children perform the actions or vice versa. Also you can ask for volunteers to tell and show the skills of Circle Time. Use stickers in the circle to commend children for using their skills.

Assessing the children's progress

As there is no suitable or appropriate test for measuring children's progress in personal, social and emotional development accurately, assessment is carried out by observation. Quality Circle Time provides the ideal forum for observing and assessing the children in your group. You need to make sure that all the practitioners involved fully understand what is expected of the children for each stepping stone, they will then be able to see where children do not meet the criteria of the designated activity. Using Circle Time observations alongside observations of a child at other times and in differing situations will provide an overall picture of that child's development. This will enable the practitioner to plan any additional support that may be required. It is important not to be too hasty with negative observations as a child may be having an off day due to feeling unwell or because of an earlier incident. Generally speaking, the majority of children will fall into a band of acceptable learning and behaviour. Those who consistently remain outside this band will, in due course, be referred for specialist assessment and support.

Setting targets in circle time

As stated earlier in this book, one of the aims of Quality Circle Time is to encourage the children to monitor and regulate their own behaviour within the group. Within the circle, children can discuss aspects of their behaviour and the impact they have on others. This makes it easier for a child to understand why certain elements of their behaviour provokes particular responses or reactions. If, for example, a child frequently snatches toys from the other children, this can be discussed during Circle Time and the other children can volunteer how it makes them feel. It is also an ideal opportunity to remind the children that snatching is breaking the Golden Rules of being kind and gentle. A target can be set from the discussion with an agreed incentive. All the children can be urged to help a child to meet their target. With the involvement and support of the whole group, there is a greater chance of achieving success. Moreover, peer pressure often has a deeper 'more lasting' effect than the admonitions of an adult.

Maintaining the quality of circle time

Circle Time provides the ideal opportunity to enhance self–esteem, deal with problems and cultural or topical issues, impart information, motivate the children to learn and encourage self–discipline. However, it will only be effective if it is a time of quality.

It is important to review the quality of your Circle Time every term to make sure that it is fulfilling the purpose intended for it. Always use a lesson plan and be clear about the learning objectives you want to promote. Whilst young children like some repetition, don't allow Circle Time to become boring or stale. Most importantly, practitioners need to be aware of, and always practise, the following Circle Time skills:

- ♦ Empathetic listening

- ♦ The use of good eye contact

- ♦ The ability to show emotional warmth

- ♦ The ability to recap and reflect back what a child has said

- ♦ The ability to respond pro-actively to negative behaviour

- ♦ The ability to use effective encouragement

- ♦ The ability to offer support appropriately

- ♦ A positive approach to the activities

If the prescribed guidelines for running Circle Time are adhered to and the quality is maintained, you will find this a powerful and motivational force in the education of your children and a great aid to attaining the early learning goals.

How to use this book

The activities in this book are divided into the six sections of personal, social and emotional development as follows:

- ◆ For dispositions and attitudes

- ◆ For self–confidence and self–esteem

- ◆ For making relationships

- ◆ For behaviour and self–control

- ◆ For self–care. (This section also includes early learning goals for health and bodily awareness from the area of Physical Development.)

- ◆ For sense of community.

Each section contains twelve lesson plans for Circle Time which progress through the yellow, blue and green stepping stones to the early learning goals. You can select the lesson plans that are appropriate for your curriculum requirements and modify them for different settings. However, the plans should be used in a developmental way and different sections should not be used in isolation.

The lesson plans inform you of any resources that you will need and give examples and suggestions to follow, although the activities can be changed or adapted to fit in with any topic you are currently studying.

Early Learning Goals for dispositions and attitudes

Yellow stepping stones

Blue stepping stones

New Beginnings

Green stepping stones

Going for goals

New Beginnings.

Early Learning Goals

Going for goals

New Beginnings.   *Getting on & falling out*

Going for goals   *New Beginnings*

Early Learning Goals for self-confidence and self-esteem

Blue stepping stones

Green stepping stones

Going for goals
Good to be me

New Beginnings   *Getting On & falling out.*

Good to be me

New beginnings   *Getting on & falling out*

Early Learning Goals

Respond to significant experiences, showing a range of feelings

[handwritten: New Beginnings / Getting on & falling out]

Have a developing awareness of their own needs, views and

[handwritten: New Beginnings / Getting on & falling out]

Have a developing respect for their own cultures and beliefs and

[handwritten: New Beginnings / Getting on & falling out]

Early Learning Goals for making relationships

Yellow stepping stones

Blue stepping stones

Demonstrate flexibility and adapt their behaviour to different events,

Green stepping stones

[handwritten: New Beginnings / Getting on & falling out]

Early Learning Goals

[handwritten: New Beginnings / Getting on & falling out]

Understand that there need to be agreed values and codes of behaviour for groups of

[handwritten: New Beginnings / Getting on & falling out]

[handwritten left margin: Bridging goals / Good to be Me / Good to be Me]

Early Learning Goals for behaviour and self-control

Yellow stepping stones

Blue stepping stones

Early Learning Goals

Early Learning Goals for self-care and health and bodily awareness

Yellow stepping stones

Blue stepping stones

Early Learning Goals

Early Learning Goals for sense of community

Yellow stepping stones

Blue stepping stones

Green stepping stones

Early Learning Goals

ELGs for dispositions and attitudes
Lesson 1

Pupils should be taught to:
Have a positive approach to new experiences
Show confidence in linking up with others for support and guidance

Resources:
None

Introductory phase:
Mime simple actions for children to follow, identifying areas of the body they are touching e.g. tap your nose, touch your toes, clap your hands, stamp your feet, click your fingers, blink your eyes, shake your shoulders, wave your elbows.

Follow with lots of praise about how well they did.

Middle phase:
A musical hello, using the traditional rhyme:

> Tommy Thumb, Tommy Thumb, Where are you?

Substitute the first two words with:
> 'Hello (...............), Hello (...............) Where are you?'

The child replies,
> 'Here I am, Here I am'.

To which you respond,
> 'How do you do!'

Smile at each child and try to engage eye contact, and perhaps a handshake
Continue around the circle until all the children have had a turn.

Repeat asking the children to help you sing. Remind them that we say 'Hello' when we meet someone. All the children can shake hands when 'How do you do' is sung.

Clap each child's name several times. Ask the group to join in. Use different tempos.

Closing phase/plenary:
Congratulate the children for trying out a new idea and for joining in so well.

A musical goodbye, using the traditional rhyme:

> 'Twinkle twinkle little star'

Sing to each child,
> 'Now it's time to say goodbye (child's name), (child's name), wave goodbye'.

Encourage the children to wave goodbye when their name is sung.

Congratulate the children for doing so well.

ELGs for dispositions and attitudes
Lesson 2

Pupils should be taught to:
Have a positive approach to new experiences
Show confidence in linking up with others for support and guidance

Resources:
A speaking object
A puppet

Introductory phase:
Clap and touch, The children copy the practitioner. The adult gives two claps and touches a part of their body with both hands, (e.g., clap, clap, touch head, clap, clap, touch knees), change the speed of clapping and touching.

Follow with lots of praise about how well they did.

Middle phase:
Introduce the puppet by name, e.g. 'Salt' to the children and then say he wants to know their names. They need to take it in turns to talk to him, the child holding the speaking object is the one whose turn it is.
They say ' Hello my name is…' Remind the children to look at the puppet when they are talking to him.

It is time for the puppet to go away, child can say goodbye to him and stroke him gently if they would like to, but they can say no if they do not want to stroke him.

The puppet is taken to each child in turn for them to say goodbye.

Closing phase/plenary:
Congratulate the children for joining in and speaking in the circle.

A musical goodbye, using the traditional rhyme:

    'Twinkle twinkle little star'.

Sing to each child
    'Now it's time to say goodbye, (child's name), (child's name), wave goodbye'.

Encourage the children to wave goodbye when their name is sung.

Congratulate the children for doing so well.

ELGs for dispositions and attitudes
Lesson 3

Pupils should be taught to:
Have a positive approach to new experiences
Show confidence in linking up with others for support and guidance

Resources:
A speaking object

Introductory phase:
A musical hello, using the traditional rhyme:

Tommy Thumb, Tommy Thumb, Where are you?

Substitute the first two words with
'Hello (…………….), Hello (……………..) Where are you?'

The child replies
'Here I am, Here I am'.

To which you respond,
'How do you do!'

Smile at each child and try to engage eye contact, and perhaps a handshake
Continue around the circle until all the children have had a turn.

Middle phase:
Remind the children that when we meet people we say 'Hello'. Everyone is going to have a turn to say 'Hello'. When they have the speaking object they say 'Hello my name is…'

Round "Hello my name is…"

Closing phase/plenary:
Congratulate children for joining in and speaking in the circle.

Animal Game The practitioner goes around the circle telling each child they are one of three animals, e.g. duck, cow, or dog. When their animal is mentioned the children make appropriate noises. When 'farmyard' is said all the animals make their noise.

ELGs for dispositions and attitudes **Lesson 4**
Pupils should be taught to: Have a positive approach to new experiences Show confidence in linking up with others for support and guidance
Resources: A speaking object A medium sized ball
Introductory phase: Mime simple actions for the children to follow, e.g., brushing teeth, playing a piano, carrying a heavy parcel, threading beads, putting on wellington boots, nursing a baby. Give lots of praise for how well they all did.
Middle phase: The children sit in the circle. Roll the ball to each child in turn saying 'Hello... and their name'. When they receive the ball, they say 'Thank you' and send it back to you saying, 'Hello... (your name) you should remember to say 'Thank you'. "We all like playing with the ball. What else do the children like to play with?" **Round** "I like to play with…"
Closing phase/plenary: Congratulate children for joining in and speaking in the circle.
Animal Game The practitioner goes around the circle telling each child they are one of three animals, e.g. duck, cow, or dog. When their animal is mentioned the children make appropriate noises. When 'farmyard' is said all the animals make their noise

ELGs for dispositions and attitudes
Lesson 5

Pupils should be taught to:
Have a positive approach to new experiences
Show confidence in linking up with others for support and guidance

Resources:
A speaking object
A medium sized ball

Introductory phase:
Roll the ball to each child in turn saying 'Hello... and their name'. When they receive the ball they say, 'Thank you' and send it back to you saying 'Hello... (your name). You should remember to say 'Thank you'.

Middle phase:
The practitioner tells the story of a little girl who only ever said ' Thank you'. When the practitioner pauses the children, supply the thank yous.

'One day there was a little girl who only ever said... she went out into the garden and shouted ... All the birds flew away so she whispered...and skipped around the garden singing... Her mother came out and said, "I wish you would say something else". The girl smiled and said "PLEASE".

Ask the children to think about when they say 'Thank you'.

Round "I say thank you when..."

Closing phase/plenary:
Congratulate the children for joining in and speaking in the circle.

Pass a smile. The practitioner smiles at the child on her right who smiles at the child on their right, until the smile has gone all around the circle.

ELGs for dispositions and attitudes **Lesson 6**
Pupils should be taught to: Display high levels of involvement in activities
Resources: Recorded sounds or actual objects (placed in a pillow case, e.g., paper to rip or screw up, bells, shaker, bean bag, tambourine, etc.) A tambourine
Introductory phase: **Name clap.** The children say the name of each child in the circle in turn. As they say the name they clap the rhythm of the name.
Middle phase: **Guess the sound.** The practitioner either plays a recorded selection of different sounds, or uses some familiar objects the children have to guess what they are. The practitioner plays a simple rhythm using the tambourine children try to clap the same rhythm.
Closing phase/plenary: **Clap and touch.** The children copy the practitioner. The practitioner gives two claps and touches a part of their body with both hands, (e.g., clap, clap, touch head, clap, clap, touch knees), change speed of clapping and touching. Follow with lots of praise about how well they did.

ELGs for dispositions and attitudes
Lesson 7

Pupils should be taught to:
Be confident to speak in a familiar group
Maintain attention, concentrate and sit quietly when appropriate

Resources:
A speaking object

Introductory phase:
A musical hello, using the traditional rhyme
   Tommy Thumb, Tommy Thumb, Where are you?
Substitute the first two words with
   'Hello (………..), Hello (………..) Where are you?'
The child replies:
   'Here I am, Here I am'.
To which you respond:
   'How do you do!'
Smile at each child and try to engage eye contact, and perhaps a handshake
Continue around the circle until all the children have had a turn.

Middle phase:
Remind the children that we say 'Hello' when we meet others.

Round "Hello my name is…"

Ask the children to think about what they like to do at home or school.

Round - "At home I like to…"
            Or
Round - "At school I like to…"

Ask for volunteers to act out another thing they like to do at home or school whilst the rest of the class try and guess what they are doing.

Closing phase/plenary:
Congratulate the children for listening to each other and for speaking so that others could hear them.

Guess who. Three or four children stand in the middle of the circle. The rest of the children close their eyes and the practitioner touches one of the children in the middle who then makes an animal noise e.g. 'quack quack'. The children in the circle try to guess which child made the noise. This can be repeated changing the children in the middle of the circle.

ELGs for dispositions and attitudes **Lesson 8**
Pupils should be taught to: Be confident to speak in a familiar group Maintain attention, concentrate and sit quietly when appropriate
Resources: A speaking object A tambourine or a large bunch of keys
Introductory phase: **Pass a smile.** The practitioner smiles at the child on their right, who then passes the smile on around the circle. Encourage eye contact.
Middle phase: Explain to the children you are going to have a round. **Round** "Hello my name is…" Tell the children you are going to see how good they are at listening. Play, 'Simon Says'. The children only do the actions when Simon tells them to e.g., 'Simon says touch your toes'. If the practitioner just says the action without 'Simon says' the children do not do the action. In turn each child tells the other children what action to do, but they put their name before the action e.g., "Anne says…"
Closing phase/plenary: Congratulate the children for listening to each other and for speaking so that others could hear them. **Silent pass.** The children try to pass a bunch of keys or a tambourine around the circle without making a noise.

**ELGs for dispositions and attitudes
Lesson 9**

Pupils should be taught to:
Be confident to speak in a familiar group
Maintain attention, concentrate and sit quietly when appropriate

Resources:
A speaking object
A tambourine or a large bunch of keys

Introductory phase:
Play oranges and lemons to ensure the children are mixed up in the circle. The children are alternately labelled "orange" or "lemon". The practitioner says either "oranges" or "lemons". The children change seats with the same fruit. If Fruit Basket is called, all the children change seats.

Middle phase:
Ask the children to think about their favourite colour.
Round. "My favourite colour is…"

Ask them why they chose their colour. (Answers may be, "Because I have a dress in that colour" or "It's the colour of the sky".)

Ask the children to think about being an animal and to choose one particular one they would like to be.
Round. "I would like to be a …"

Ask them why they chose to be their particular animal.

Closing phase/plenary:
Congratulate the children for listening to each other and for speaking so that others could hear them.

Silent pass. The children try to pass a bunch of keys or a tambourine around the circle without making a noise.

ELGs for dispositions and attitudes
Lesson 10

Pupils should be taught to:
Be confident to speak in a familiar group
Maintain attention, concentrate and sit quietly when appropriate

Resources:
A speaking object

Introductory phase:
Play oranges and lemons to ensure the children are mixed up in the circle. The children are alternately labelled "orange" or "lemon". The practitioner says either "oranges" or "lemons". The children change seats with the same fruit. If Fruit Basket is called, all the children change seats.

Middle phase:
Ask children to think about what they did before coming to school that day, e.g., got up, washed, ate breakfast etc.

Ask for volunteers to act out what they did before school.

Round. "Before I came to school I…"

What will they do after school?

Round. "After school I will…"

Closing phase/plenary:
Congratulate the children for listening to each other and for speaking so that others could hear them.

Reflections. The children copy the practitioner's simple actions. Use some actions expressed by the children in the rounds, e.g., brushing teeth, eating breakfast, getting dressed, playing with friends, watching TV.

ELGs for dispositions and attitudes
Lesson 11

Pupils should be taught to:
Be confident to speak in a familiar group
Maintain attention, concentrate and sit quietly when appropriate

Resources:
A speaking object
A rain stick or mood music

Introductory phase:
Reflections. The children copy the practitioners' simple actions, e.g., miming, brushing teeth, eating breakfast, getting dressed, reading a book, painting a picture, making a model, nursing a baby, threading beads.

Middle phase:
Ask the children what they need to do, to be good at reflections i.e., look, think, concentrate.

When do the children need to do these things in school?

What makes it hard to look, think, and concentrate?

Ask the children what they like to look at, (no TV programmes!)
Round. "I like to look at..."

What do they like to think about?
Round. "I like to think about... "
(You may have to start this round.)

Closing phase/plenary:
Congratulate children for listening to each other and for speaking so that others could hear them.

Explain that you are going to give the children time to think their happy thoughts.
The children close their eyes and put their hands on their knees with the palms facing upwards and their fingers slightly curled. This relaxes their shoulders and most children find it easier to sit very still in this position. Using a rain stick or a mood music tape allow the children to listen and think their happy thoughts.

Whilst their happy thoughts are still in their minds pass a smile. The practitioner smiles at the child on their right, who then passes the smile on around the circle. Remember eye contact.

ELGs for dispositions and attitudes
Lesson 12

Pupils should be taught to:
Be confident to speak in a familiar group
Maintain attention, concentrate and sit quietly when appropriate

Resources:
A speaking object
A small ball
A bunch of keys
A blindfold or scarf
A rain stick or mood music

Introductory phase:
I know your name. Calling out the name of the recipient, a child rolls the ball to them, the game continues until all the children have had a turn. Children should fold their arms when they have had a turn.

Middle phase:
The practitioner asks the children to close their eyes and listen to any sounds they can hear.

Round "I could hear…"

Where are the keys? One child is blindfolded. A large bunch of keys or some other noisy object is passed around the circle, as quietly as possible. The child, in the centre of the circle with the blindfold on must listen and try to identify where the keys are and then shout 'Stop' pointing in that direction. After two guesses, another child takes their place in the centre.

Remember to praise the child in the middle for trying even if they can't locate the sound of the keys.

What sound/noise do you like to listen to?
Round "I like to listen to…"

Closing phase/plenary:
Congratulate the children for listening to each other and for speaking so that others could hear them.

Explain that you are going to play mood music or use the rain stick for children to imagine a scene in which things change, e.g., playing in the park, swimming in the sea.

Ask which children would like to share their thoughts/visualisation with the rest of the class.

Further activities and strategies for dispositions and attitudes

♦ Give positive feedback.

♦ Provide open-ended materials that appeal to children's senses e.g. soapy sand, tray of buttons, coloured water, play dough.

♦ Encourage the children to complete a task before moving to another.

♦ Provide the opportunity for the children to repeat tasks until they succeed.

♦ Observe the children engaged in self-chosen activities and use this information in your planning.

♦ Develop routines that encourage independence:

  ♦ self registration

  ♦ labelled places for children's property

  ♦ silhouettes or labels so that the children can return resources to appropriate

  ♦ places

  ♦ teach skills needed for personal hygiene, dressing and undressing

  ♦ involve the children in decision making about routines.

♦ Encourage the children to help each other rather than always seeking adult help.

♦ Limit numbers in activities by having the right number of aprons, silhouettes for shoes, near to sandpit etc.

♦ Encourage the children to plan how they will complete an activity.

♦ Provide activities that encourage the children to ask questions and solve problems.

♦ Ensure that adult directed activities have choices within them.

♦ Accept the children's own choices.

♦ Prepare the children for new activities and changes in routine.

♦ Provide opportunities for the children to work in groups/pairs/alone.

♦ Provide appropriate and well-resourced role-play.

♦ Work closely with parents/carers. Let them know your plans for each half term.

ELGs for self-confidence and self-esteem **Lesson 1**
Pupils should be taught to: Have a sense of belonging
Resources: None
Introductory phase: **Name clap** The children say the name of each child in the circle in turn. As they say the name they clap the rhythm of the name. Congratulate them for knowing each others' names.

Middle phase:
Sing the 'Belonging Song', to the tune of 'The wheels on the bus'.
 	
    Children in this class/group like to play, like to play, like to play.
    Children in this class/group like to play, all day long.
 	
Add verses that mention children by name and let the child choose their own activity, e.g.,
    Nazra in this class/group likes to skip,
    Leon in this class/group likes to paint,
 	
Involve as many individual children as possible. Actions can be added.
 	
Ask the children how many of them like to do the activities mentioned in the song. Call out the actions one at a time and children put their thumbs up if they do.

Closing phase/plenary: Congratulate the children for doing so well. **Pass a smile** The practitioner smiles at the child on her right who smiles at the child on their right, until the smile has gone all around the circle.

ELGs for self-confidence and self-esteem
Lesson 2

Pupils should be taught to:
Have a sense of belonging

Resources:
A speaking object
A puppet

Introductory phase:
Listen and touch – practitioner tells children to touch a part of their body, or object with their thumb, little finger, elbow etc. E.g. touch the floor with your elbow, touch your teeth with your little finger, touch your nose with your thumb.

Middle phase:
Introduce the puppet, e.g., Salt who tells the children why he likes being in the class/group and about some of the things he likes to do, e.g., listen to a story, play outside, build with the Lego, paint a picture, play with his friends.

Ask the children to think of something they like to do in the class/group.
Round "I like to…"
             Or
Round   "At pre-school/nursery I like to…"

Closing phase/plenary:
Congratulate the children for doing so well.

End by singing together, 'If you're happy and you know it'

If you're happy and you know it…Clap your hands, Stamp your feet, Shout, 'I am'
If you're happy and you know it and you really want to show it,
If you're happy and you know it…

ELGs for self-confidence and self-esteem
Lesson 3

Pupils should be taught to:
Show care and concern for self

Resources:
A speaking object
A puppet

Introductory phase:
Name clap The children say the name of each child in the circle in turn. As they say the name they clap the rhythm of the name.

Congratulate them for knowing each others' names.

Middle phase:
The puppet tells the children his/her name and lots of things he/she can do, e.g., "I'm Salt and I can: run, shout, walk, eat my dinner, wash my hands, paint a picture."

Ask the children to think of all the things that they can do but in the round they are only going to say one.

Round "I'm ... and I can..."

Ask if any child can think of anything that they need help to do?

If no one can think you could suggest, crossing the road, buttoning their coats, tying their shoe laces etc.

Closing phase/plenary:
Congratulate the children for doing so well.

Train game The children listen and copy the rhythm. Start the chant slowly and gradually build up speed and momentum, like a train pulling away from a station platform, until the final "**soup**" sounds like the train whistle.

   Water, water, water, water,
   Cheese and biscuits, (x 4)
   Chocolate pudding, (x 4)
   Fish and chips , (x 4)
   SOOOOUP!!!!

Words can be changed to fit in with your topic, e.g., 'Three Little Pigs, can be used as house of straw (x 3), house of sticks, (x 3) house of bricks, (x 3) with WOLF being used as the whistle.

ELGs for self-confidence and self-esteem **Lesson 4**
Pupils should be taught to: Show care and concern for self
Resources: A speaking object
Introductory phase: **Pass a smile**   The practitioner smiles at the child on her right who smiles at the child on their right, until the smile has gone all around the circle. Encourage the children to make eye contact. Explain when we smile we all look happy.
Middle phase: Sing the song, 'If you're happy and you know it'. If you're happy and you know it…Clap your hands, Stamp your feet, Shout, 'I am' If you're happy and you know it and you really want to show it If you're happy and you know it… Ask the children to think about what makes them happy. **Round** "I am happy when…" Suggest things that might make them happy, e.g., eating burger and chips, listening to a story, painting a picture, playing with their friends, having a hug. If the children agree, they put their thumbs up.

Closing phase/plenary:
Congratulate the children for doing so well.
 	
Aiken Drum Faces Change the words after the chorus
 	
Chorus
     'There was a man lived in the moon, lived in the moon, lived in the moon,
     There was a man lived in the moon and his name was Aiken Drum.'
 	
     His face was always… sad, angry, excited, happy etc. (x 3)
     His face was always …sad, etc., and his name was Aiken Drum.
 	
Ask the children to make their faces and voices fit the words in the song. Always finish with happy!

ELGs for self-confidence and self-esteem **Lesson 5**
Pupils should be taught to: Talk freely about their home and community
Resources: A speaking object Two puppets
Introductory phase: **Labels** Alternately label the children. You could use suitable words from your topic, e.g., cat/dog, red/blue, square/circle. The practitioner calls out one of the labels and all the children with that label have to stand up. It works well if you try to trick them by repeating the same label. Wait until all the children are sitting down and ready before calling out the next label.
Middle phase: Introduce the puppets who tell the children that they are brother/sister or two brothers/sisters and they live together, e.g., Salt and Pepper. Salt: Hello my name is Salt. Pepper: Hello my name is Pepper and Salt is my brother. Salt: Pepper is my sister. Together: We live together. Salt: We live with our Gran and our Mum and our Dad   . Ask the children to think about who they live with. **Round**   "I live with…" Be sensitive to children's different families. The puppets tell the children some of the things they do at home, e.g., play with their toys, watch TV, read stories, eat, go to bed.   If the children do these things they should put their thumbs up. Ask the children to think about one thing they do at home. **Round** "At home I…"
Closing phase/plenary: Congratulate the children for doing so well and telling us about what they do at home. Mime simple actions for children to follow, some fast, some slow, e.g., brushing hair, cleaning teeth, walking up stairs, having their tea, watching TV, listening to a story, having a hug. Give lots of praise for how well they all did.

ELGs for self-confidence and self-esteem
Lesson 6

Pupils should be taught to:
Talk freely about their home and community

Resources:
A speaking object
Two puppets

Introductory phase:
Labels Alternately label the children. You could use suitable words from your topic, e.g., cat/dog, red/blue, square/circle. The practitioner calls out one of the labels and all the children with that label have to stand up. It works well if you try to trick them by repeating the same label. Wait until all the children are sitting down and ready before calling out the next label.

Middle phase:
Introduce the puppets who give examples of what they do when they are not in the group, e.g., go to the park, shop, visit other people, play with friends, go to church. Children put their thumbs up if they do those things.

Ask the children to think about something they do when they are not in the group.

Round "When I am not in the group I ..."

Closing phase/plenary:
Congratulate the children for doing so well and telling us about what they do.

Clap and touch. The children copy the practitioner. The practitioner gives two claps and touches a part of her body with both hands, (e.g., clap, clap, touch head, clap, clap, touch knees). Change the speed of clapping and touching.

ELGs for self- confidence and self-esteem
Lesson 7

Pupils should be taught to:
Have a sense of self as a member of different communities

Resources:
A speaking object
Mood music - happy

Introductory phase:
Sing the 'Belonging Song; to the tune of 'The wheels on the bus'.

    Children in this class/group like to play, like to play, like to play.
    Children in this class/group like to play, all day long.

Add verses that mention children by name and let the child choose their own activity e.g.,
    Jill in this class/group likes to skip,
    Ben in this class/group likes to paint,

Involve as many individual children as possible. Actions can be added.

Middle phase:
Tell the children we all belong to this class/group. Can anyone think of another group they belong to?

If the children find this difficult give them ideas: family, school , church, swimming club, etc.

Round "I belong to…"

Are there any groups that they would like to belong to when they are older? e.g., Rainbows, Beavers etc.

Explain that usually if you are in a group you feel happy with the rest of the group and you all smile at each other.

Closing phase/plenary:
Smiling can make other people feel happy, so this week all of the class/group is going to smile as much as possible!

The children close their eyes and put their hands on their knees with the palms facing upwards and their fingers slightly curled. This relaxes their shoulders and most children find it easier to sit very still in this position. Using a mood music tape encourages children to close their eyes and listen to the music. Ask the class if the music made them feel happy? Finish the lesson by listening to more of the happy music.

ELGs for self-confidence and self-esteem
Lesson 8

Pupils should be taught to:
Respond to significant experiences, showing a range of feelings when appropriate

Resources:
A speaking object
Pictures of children's faces showing different feelings
Mood music

Introductory phase:
Pass a smile The practitioner smiles at the child on their right, who then passes the smile on around the circle. Encourage eye contact.

Explain that our faces can show how we are feeling. Ask the children to make a sad face.

Middle phase:
Using the pictures ask the children if they can tell how the children are feeling by looking at their faces?

Ask the children to make a happy face, an angry face, a surprised face, a frightened face, an excited face. Volunteers could show their faces to the rest of the class.

Using the pictures (one at a time), ask why the children on the pictures might be feeling the way they look.
Round   "I think the girl/boy is feeling sad (or which ever feeling you use) because…"

Ask if anyone has felt sad and what made him or her feel sad?

The round and the telling can be repeated several times using various pictures.

Closing phase/plenary:
Reassure the children that we have different feelings and it is OK to show your feelings but sometimes we have to control our feelings. Can anybody think when they had to control their feelings? The adult may have to give their example first.

The children close their eyes and put their hands on their knees with the palms facing upwards and their fingers slightly curled. This relaxes their shoulders and most children find it easier to sit very still in this position. Using a mood music tape encourages children to close their eyes and listen to the music. Play music to evoke different feelings, after each short piece stop and ask the children how the music makes them feel.

ELGs for self-confidence and self-esteem
Lesson 9

Pupils should be taught to:
Express needs and feelings in appropriate ways
Have a developing awareness of their own needs, views and feelings and be sensitive to the needs, views and feelings of others

Resources:
A speaking object
Photographs of children at different ages – birth up to 4 year old
A baby or doll

Introductory phase:
Clap and touch The children copy the practitioner. The practitioner gives two claps and touches a part of her body with both hands, (e.g., clap, clap, touch head, clap, clap, touch knees), change speed of clapping and touching.

Middle phase:
Use a photograph of a new baby, or a doll, or a real baby. Ask the children what a new baby needs?

Look at the photograph of a two-year-old. Ask what things did they learn to do when they were two?
Ask what a two-year-old needs?

Look at the four year old photograph and ask the children to think about what they need now they are four or five.

Round "Now I am four/five I need…"
If food, drink, sleep, exercise, love, care are not mentioned bring them to the circle.

Closing phase/plenary:
Remind the children that we all have needs, they change as we get older but we all need: food, drink, sleep, exercise, love, care.

Congratulate the children for joining in and speaking in the circle.

Name clap All the children clap twice and then say the name of a child, e.g., clap, clap, Jessica. Continue around the circle until all the children have had a turn at being named.

ELGs for self-confidence and self-esteem
Lesson 10

Pupils should be taught to:
Have a developing awareness of their own needs, views and feelings and be sensitive to the needs, views and feelings of others

Resources:
A speaking object

Introductory phase:
Simon says Use body part names in the game, e.g., "Simon says look at your knees," "Simon says tap your shoulder with one hand". The children should not do the action if Simon doesn't say.

Middle phase:
This lesson we are thinking about the good things we can do with parts of our body.

This is a long list of Rounds. Choose the ones more appropriate for your group.

Round "With my hands I can…"

Ask if there are any bad/wrong things people do with their hands.

Round "With my feet I can…"

What bad/wrong things can people do with their feet?

Round "With my eyes I like to look at…"

Round "With my ears I like to hear…"

Closing phase/plenary:
Thank the children for sharing their views, ideas, and stress that although they may be different from other children's they are right for them. We don't all like the same things and we are not all good at the same things. We are all unique and different.

Clap and touch The children copy the practitioner. The practitioner gives two claps and touches a part of her body with both hands, (e.g., clap, clap, touch head, clap, clap, touch knees), change speed of clapping and touching.

ELGs for self-confidence and self-esteem
Lesson 11

Pupils should be taught to:
Have a developing respect for their own cultures and beliefs and those of other people

Resources:
A speaking object
Music that can be stopped and started

Introductory phase:
Sing together, 'If you're happy and you know it'

If you're happy and you know it...Clap your hands, Stamp your feet, Shout, 'I am'
If you're happy and you know it and you really want to show it
If you're happy and you know it...

Middle phase:
Explain to the children that we often sing when we are celebrating. Ask the children to think about celebrations that happen in school. What do we celebrate in school? They may need adult prompting.

Ask what the children celebrate in their own homes.
Round "We celebrate…."
Make a list of the celebrations that the children mention.

Ask the children to think about how they celebrate, i.e., do they have presents, sing special songs, eat special food?
Round "When we celebrate…. we…"

Ask for volunteers to act out some of the things they do when celebrating.

Closing phase/plenary:
Thank the children for sharing their celebrations, we don't all do the same things but we all enjoy celebrations.

Tell the children we are going to end with a game that could be played at a party or a celebration.

Musical statues with mime. The children stand and the practitioner gives them a task to do e.g., cleaning their teeth, whilst the music is played. When the music stops they must freeze. Anyone who moves is out and sits down.

ELGs for self-confidence and self-esteem
Lesson 12

Pupils should be taught to:
Have a developing respect for their own cultures and beliefs and those of other people

Resources:
A speaking object
A candle or a night light in a safe holder

Introductory phase:
Pass a smile The practitioner smiles at the child on their right, who then passes the smile on around the circle. Encourage eye contact

Middle phase:
Explain that different religions have different celebrations but often they involve light. Light the candle in the middle of the circle.

Depending on the beliefs of the children in your class, you may have to introduce some variety into the circle. You should aim to mention Hindu, (Divali), Christian, (Christmas), Islam, (Ramadan), Judaism, (Hanukkah).

Ask the children to think about which religious festival they celebrate
Round "I celebrate…"

How do they celebrate?
Round "When it is … we…"

Ask for volunteers to act out some things they do when celebrating. Be aware of the candle or night light. You may have to blow it out for this part of the lesson!

Closing phase/plenary:
Thank the children for sharing their celebrations, we don't all do the same things but we all enjoy celebrations.

Ask the children to look at the lighted candle and think of the good times they have when they celebrate. Blow out the candle.

Pass a friendly squeeze The practitioner squeezes the hand of one of the children sitting next to her, who passes it on to the next child, and so on around the circle until the squeeze is passed back to the practitioner.

Further activities and strategies for self-confidence and self-esteem

♦ Comprehensive induction programme

♦ Work closely with parents/carers

♦ Model appropriate language and reaction to others

♦ Encourage children to speak in front of others

♦ Ensure the children know each other's names

♦ Encourage the children to give messages to other adults or their peers

♦ Ensure that tasks are challenging but achievable

♦ Encourage the children to talk about their homes

♦ Role-play related to children's home

♦ Role-play related to other cultures

♦ Celebrate cultural and religious festivals

♦ Arrange cultural events

♦ Read appropriate stories and poems depicting feelings

♦ Organise activities that allow the children to express their feelings e.g. moving to music, singing, listening to music, making music, painting, drama, puppets, and small world etc

♦ Allow the children to show their feelings. Don't always try to 'jolly them along' if they are feeling unhappy. Tell them that you understand and give them time to recover.

♦ Encourage parents/carers to bring young babies into the setting

♦ Ask children to help serve snacks and other routine jobs

♦ Value children's 'work' and if there is an end product, display it appropriately. Take photographs of models.

♦ Organise 'Star of the week'. Each child has a turn at being the star or the chosen one. They bring in things from home to show to the group. A certificate or a rosette can be given to the 'star'.

ELGs for making relationships
Lesson 1

Pupils should be taught to:
Relate and make attachments to members of the group

Resources:
None

Introductory phase:
Animal game – The practitioner goes around the circle telling each child they are one of three animals, e.g. duck, cow, or dog. When their animal is mentioned the children make appropriate noises. When 'farmyard' is said all the animals make their noise.
The game can be varied by asking children to make the noises sound: sad, cross, happy, etc.

Middle phase:
The practitioner shakes hands with the child on her left or right and says 'Hello…' The hello shake is passed around the circle until it comes back to the practitioner.

Sing the 'Belonging Song', to the tune of 'The wheels on the bus'.

    Children in this class/group like to play, like to play, like to play.
    Children in this class/group like to play, all day long.

Add verses that mention children by name and let the children choose their own activity, e.g.,
    Jill in this class/group likes to skip,
    Ben in this class/group likes to paint,

Involve as many individual children as possible. Actions can be added.

Closing phase/plenary:
Congratulate the children for joining in.

Name clap The children say the name of each child in the circle in turn. As they say the name they clap the rhythm of the name.

ELGs for making relationships
Lesson 2

Pupils should be taught to:
Relate and make attachments to members of the group

Resources:
None

Introductory phase:
A musical hello using the traditional rhyme:

Tommy Thumb, Tommy Thumb, Where are you?

Substitute the first two words with;
'Hello (………..), Hello (………) Where are you?'

The child replies;
'Here I am, Here I am'.

To which you respond;
'How do you do!'

Smile at each child and try to engate eye contact, and perhaps a handshake. Continue around the circle until all the children have had a turn.

Repeat asking the children to help you sing. Remind them that we say 'hello' when we meet someone. All the children can shake hands when 'How do you do' is sung.

Middle phase:
Sing the 'Belonging Song', to the tune of 'The wheels on the bus'.

Children in this class/group like to play, like to play, like to play.
Children in this class/group like to play, all day long.

Add verses that mention children by name and let the children choose their own activity e.g.,
Jill in this class/group likes to skip,
Ben in this class/group likes to paint,

Involve as many individual children as possible. Actions can be added.

Closing phase/plenary:
Congratulate the children for joining in.

Catch a smile All the children and the practitioner stand up. The practitioner makes eye contact with a child and then smiles. The smiled at child smiles and sits down. Continue until everyone has had a turn.

ELGs for making relationships
Lesson 3

Pupils should be taught to:
Demonstrate flexibility and adapt their behaviour to different events, social situations and changes in routines

Resources:
A speaking object

Introductory phase:
Labels Alternately label the children. You could use suitable words from your topic, e.g. cat/dog, red/blue, square/circle. The practitioner calls out one of the labels and all the children with that label have to stand up and change places.

Depending on the behaviour of the children as they play the game, talk about playing gently and not pushing each other. There is always a spare seat. If you need to, play again with appropriate behaviour.

Middle phase:
Explain that in this lesson we are thinking about how we should behave in different places and at different times.

First of all think about a time when we really need to listen.
Round "I need to listen…"
If the children find this difficult give them some guidance; story time, register, to my teacher, to my mum, to my friend, etc.

Now think of a place where you like to run and jump and shout
Round "I like to run/jump/shout…"

Would it be a good idea to run or jump in the nursery/school building, on the park, on the road, in a shop? The children put thumbs up for good places, down for bad. Use places that reflect your situation and stress the safety aspect.

Closing phase/plenary:
Congratulate the children for joining in.

Tell the children we are going to play a game where they need to listen.
Simon says Use body part names in game, e.g. "Simon says look at your knees," "Simon says tap your shoulder with one hand." The children should not do the action if Simon doesn't say.

ELGs for making relationships
Lesson 4

Pupils should be taught to:
Value and contribute to own well-being and self-control

Resources:
A speaking object
A large picture of a baby or a baby like doll
A puppet

Introductory phase:
Labels Alternately label the children, you could use suitable words from your topic, e.g., cat/dog, red/blue, square/circle. The practitioner calls out one of the labels and all the children with that label have to stand up and change places.

Depending on the behaviour of the children, as they play the game, talk about playing gently and not pushing each other. There is always a spare seat. If you need to, play again with appropriate behaviour.

Middle phase:
Congratulate the children for listening and for playing the game so well.

Show the picture or the doll. Explain that when the children were babies, they didn't know how to play games and listen. If they wanted something like food or a hug, all they could do was cry. Now you are learning to do many things for yourself. Can you think of something you have learnt to do?
Round "I have learnt to…"

Make a list of all the things they have learnt to do: listen, talk, walk, run, jump, paint, draw, dance, share, care, say sorry, etc.

Closing phase/plenary:
Congratulate the children for joining in.

Tell the children they are going to show everyone that they have learnt how to be gentle. Show the puppet and say that they can say goodbye to the puppet by gently stroking him. The children have a right to say "NO," if they do not want to stroke the puppet. Take the puppet to each child and let them say goodbye and stroke him gently if they wish.

ELGs for making relationships
Lesson 5

Pupils should be taught to:
Value and contribute to own well-being and self-control

Resources:
A speaking object

Introductory phase:
Reflections   The children copy the practitioner's simple actions, e.g., brushing teeth, eating, painting a picture, waving and smiling.

Middle phase:
Congratulate the children for looking carefully and for copying the actions so well.

Catch a smile All the children and the practitioner stand up. The practitioner makes eye contact with a child and then smiles. The smiled at child smiles and sits down. Continue until everyone has had a turn.

We have all just smiled, how do you feel when people smile at you?

Round "When people smile at me I feel…."

If you smile at people you can make them feel happy. Its good to smile and make our family and friends feel happy

What things that you do make others feel sad/cross?
(Deal with any issues that come from your group)

Closing phase/plenary:
Tell the children that this week you want them to see how many people they can make feel happy.

Sing 'If you're happy and you know it clap your hands.'

If you're happy and you know it…Clap your hands, Stamp your feet, Shout, 'I am'
If you're happy and you know it and you really want to show it
If you're happy and you know it…

ELGs for making relationships
Lesson 6

Pupils should be taught to:
Value and contribute to own well-being and self-control

Resources:
A speaking object
A tambourine or a large bunch of keys

Introductory phase:
Copy a ripple   The practitioner wiggles her fingers explaining that she is making rain. The children copy. The practitioner changes the action to thunder, slapping her knees, or wind, waving her arms. The practitioner performs the various movements with her hands and ends by bringing out the sun, miming a circle with her hands. Everyone smiles.

Middle phase:
Congratulate the children for watching carefully and for playing the game so well.

Ask the children if they know what a robot is?
Robots do exactly as they are told, they are machines. The children are going to pretend to be robots. All stand up, walk around, stop, sit down, etc.

We are not like robots. We choose how we behave, and sometimes it can be hard to do what is right. If you are playing and your Mum wants you to go to bed what might you do?

If you are near a busy road how should you behave?

Round "If I am near a busy road I should..."
If your friend wants to play one game and you want to play another what might you do?

You can use relevant examples of behaviour for your group.

Closing phase/plenary:
Now we are going to play a game where you need to be quiet and careful.

Silent pass The children try to pass a bunch of keys or a tambourine around the circle without making a noise.

ELGs for making relationships
Lesson 7

Pupils should be taught to:
Form good relationships with peers

Resources:
A speaking object

Introductory phase:
Catch a smile All the children and the practitioner stand up. The practitioner makes eye contact with a child and then smiles. The smiled at child smiles back and sits down. Continue until everyone has had a turn.

Middle phase:
We have all just smiled at each other, how do you feel when people smile at you?
Round "I feel…"

If you smile at people you can make them feel happy.

It's good to make our friends feel happy. What can you do to make your friends happy?
Round "I make my friends happy …"

Ask if anyone can think of behaviour that might make a friend sad?
e.g., fighting, name calling, not sharing

Think about what you like to do with your friends.
Round "With my friends I like to…" (if the answer is 'play' try and extend it).

Closing phase/plenary:
This week try and act in a way that makes your friends happy.

Friend chant The practitioner starts the chant by clapping and chanting, "I like….", naming a child in the class. The child replies; I like … naming another child. The practitioner repeats the chant until all the children have had a turn.

ELGs for making relationships
Lesson 8

Pupils should be taught to:
Form good relationships with peers

Resources:
A speaking object
The poem 'New Friend' from 'Poems for Circle Time and Literacy Hour' LDA.

Introductory phase:
Pass-a-toe The children stand up in the circle. At first they join hands, then drop hands. The practitioner says that instead of a smile we are going to pass different parts of our body around the circle. Start with toes; children gently touch the toe of the child, next to them in the circle, with their toe. When everyone has had a turn repeat with knees, thumbs, elbows, fingertips, etc. End with a smile followed by a clap for everyone.

Middle phase:
The practitioner asks the children to think about what they have done with their friends today.
Round Today I … with my friends.

Read the poem 'New Friend' and ask the children if they have ever felt lonely because their friend was away.

Ask the children to listen to the poem again and see if you can work out what the girl did when she wanted to make a new friend, e.g. stood next to the girl she wanted to play with, asked her name, said 'Hello,' waited for the new friend to smile and talk to her.

Ask if some of the children have friends who are far away.
How do they keep in touch with friends who are far away?

Closing phase/plenary:
Friends really enjoy being together, but if you see someone looking lonely like the girl in our poem, don't forget to smile because they might like to play with you as well.

Pass a handshake and a hello The practitioner smiles at one of the children next to her, shakes their hand, and says "Hello". This is passed around the circle until it gets back to the practitioner.

ELGs for making relationships
Lesson 9

Pupils should be taught to:
Understand that there need to be agreed values and codes of behaviour for groups of people, including adults and children, to work together harmoniously.

Resources:
A speaking object
Two puppets
A small selection of toys

Introductory phase:
Play oranges and lemons to ensure children are mixed up in the circle. The children are alternately labelled "Orange" or "Lemon." The practitioner says either "oranges" or "lemons" and the children change seats with the same fruit. If "Fruit Basket" is called, all the children change seats.

Middle phase:
Congratulate the children for listening to the rules and playing the game so well. Ask them where else we have rules.

Explain that rules help everyone to feel happy and safe. That is why we have rules in school. During the next few Circle Time lessons we are going to think about our school rules or Golden Rules.

Our first Golden Rule is 'Do be gentle, do not hurt anybody'
What does "Do be gentle" mean?

The second Golden Rule is 'Do be kind and helpful, do not hurt people's feelings'

Introduce the puppets to the children, e.g., Salt and Pepper. If you have had an incident of children not being kind and helpful use that, if not use the following scenario.

Salt has a selection of toys to play with in front of him. Play out the following dialogue.

Pepper:	Can I play with you, Salt?
Salt:	No. Go away
Pepper:	Please can I play with you?
Salt:	Go away. I don't want to play with you, you are a cry baby'.

Ask the children how they think Pepper feels.
Round "Pepper feels…"

Closing phase/plenary:
Tell the children that this week you will be looking for children being gentle and kind and helpful and would like pictures of children doing gentle, kind or helpful things. (It is a good idea to have a display about the rules.)

Ask the children who in the class is gentle and never hurts others.

Ask if the children would like to show they can be gentle by saying goodbye to Pepper and gently stroking her. The children have a right to say "NO."

ELGs for making relationships
Lesson 10

Pupils should be taught to:
Understand that there need to be agreed values and codes of behaviour for groups of people, including adults and children, to work together harmoniously.

Resources:
A speaking object
Two puppets

Introductory phase:
Pass a handshake The practitioner shakes the hand of one of the children sitting next to her, who passes it on to the next child, and so on around the circle until all the children have had a turn.

Middle phase:
Congratulate them for doing it so gently and ask them to think about what they did to be gentle or kind or helpful this week.
Round "I was gentle/kind/helpful when…"
If you have noticed children behaving in this way reinforce their behaviour by praising them.

This lesson's first Golden Rule is 'Do work hard, do not waste your or other people's time'

Introduce the puppets to the children, e.g. Salt and Pepper.
If you have had an incident of children not working hard use that, if not use the following scenario.

Salt is working hard and Pepper comes and sits next to him.

Pepper: Salt can you help me with my work?
Salt: Salt looks at Pepper's work and says the answer is 5
Pepper: Have you got a rubber?
Salt: No, leave me alone I want to finish my work.

Pepper wanders off to look for a rubber and then decides to go to the toilet. She messes around in the toilet and eventually comes back to sit near Salt. It is now playtime and Salt has finished his work but Pepper has not.

Ask how does Salt feel. How does Pepper feel?

Another Golden Rule is 'Do look after property'

Using any lost property explain that Salt has lost his hat/sweatshirt. Look through the lost property trying to find one that fits, (children particularly like it when a large hat is tried on.) Explain how important it is to look after their own property.

Ask what other property they should look after.
Round "I should look after…"

Closing phase/plenary:
Remind the class you will be looking for children that are working hard and looking after property.

Mime pass Pretend to pass various things around the circle e.g., a kitten, a precious vase, a snake, a heavy case.

ELGs for making relationships
Lesson 11

Pupils should be taught to:
Understand that there need to be agreed values and codes of behaviour for groups of people, including adults and children, to work together harmoniously.

Resources:
A speaking object
Two puppets
A tambourine or a large bunch of keys

Introductory phase:
Slightly change the words of nursery rhymes e.g. Jack and hill went up the pill, Humpty Dumpty sat on a ball. The children have to repeat the correct version.

Round I like to listen to…

Middle phase:
Our first Golden Rule today is 'Do listen to people, do not interrupt'
Ask the children what "interrupt" means?

Ask the children to listen to the next Golden Rule with no one interrupting.

'Do be honest, do not cover up the truth'

Using the puppets act out a scene to illustrate being honest. If an incident regarding honesty has happened in your setting use that, otherwise:

Salt and Pepper are playing when Pepper knocks off and breaks Mum's vase.

Salt:	You should tell Mum
Pepper:	No, I'll get into trouble
Salt:	What are you going to do then
Pepper:	I'll hide the pieces under the sofa

A few days later Mum finds the pieces

Mum:	Who broke my vase?
Salt and Pepper:	It wasn't me. It wasn't me.

Mum looks at them and frowns.

Pepper:　　　Oh, I'm sorry Mum it was me, I did it.

How does Pepper feel?

Why is it sometimes difficult to be honest?
Round "It is sometimes difficult to he honest…"

Congratulate the children for listening and not interrupting.

Closing phase/plenary:
Remind the class you will be looking for children that are listening and being honest.

Silent pass The children try to pass a bunch of keys or a tambourine around the circle without making a noise.

ELGs for making relationships **Lesson 12**
Pupils should be taught to: Understand that there need to be agreed values and codes of behaviour for groups of people, including adults and children, to work together harmoniously.
Resources: A speaking object
Introductory phase: **Labels** Alternately label the children, you could use suitable words from your topic, e.g. cat/dog, red/blue, square/circle or you could use three or four labels e.g., bus/car/lorry/train. The practitioner calls out one of the labels and all the children with that label have to stand up and change seats.
Middle phase: Encourage the children to think about the Golden Rules. **Round** "A Golden Rule I know is…"   The children name one rule Congratulate the children for remembering the Golden Rules. Why do we need rules in school? i.e., to keep everyone feeling happy and safe. Ask where else we need to have rules. **Round** "We need rules…" Discuss places that have safety rules e.g., roads, swimming pools.
Closing phase/plenary: Congratulate the children for learning so much about the Golden Rules and for thinking about keeping everyone in school safe and happy. Hold hands and sing to the tune of 'London Bridge is Falling Down,' "We will keep our Golden Rules, Golden Rules, Golden Rules, We will keep our Golden Rules, to make our class/group/school happy."

Further activities and strategies for making relationships

♦ Establish routines with predictable sequences of events.

♦ Ensure each child and their carer is welcomed into the group each day and said goodbye to at the end of the session.

♦ Provide activities that involve turn taking or collaboration:

  ♦ Role play

  ♦ Small world

  ♦ Musical games

  ♦ Construction – especially with very large models

  ♦ Small apparatus, i.e., balls, quoits

  ♦ Large apparatus, i.e., see-saws, climbing frames, wheeled toys

  ♦ Floor play, including large jigsaws

  ♦ Looking at books

  ♦ Sand and water play

♦ Read appropriate stories and poems, including some where conflicts are resolved.

♦ Give practice in resolving conflict.

♦ Display group rules, including children's interpretation of the rules.

♦ Ensure parents/carers know the rules of the setting.

♦ Plan for the children to work in different sized groups, with and without adult input.

ELGs for behaviour and self-control
Lesson 1

Pupils should be taught to:
Begin to accept the needs of others, with support

Resources:
A puppet
A speaking object

Introductory phase:
Catch a smile All the children and the practitioner stand up. The practitioner makes eye contact with a child and then smiles. The smiled at child smiles back and sits down. Continue until everyone has had a turn.

Middle phase:
Introduce the puppet and tell the children that he is feeling sad.

Ask why he might be feeling sad?

Then ask the puppet who says 'he is being left out of games and no one listens to him.' Ask the children what they could do to help him.

Round "I could……"

Can the children make their faces look sad? Now change to looking very happy.

Closing phase/plenary:
Explain to the children that we want all the children and adults in our group to feel happy so we should try to help each other to feel happy.

Copy a ripple The practitioner wiggles her fingers explaining that she is making rain. The children copy. The practitioner changes the action to thunder, slapping her knees, or wind, waving her arms. The practitioner performs the various movements with her hands and ends by bringing out the sun by miming a circle with her hands. Everyone smiles.

Sing 'If you're happy and you know it'

"If you're happy and you know it…Clap your hands, Stamp your feet, Shout, 'I am'
If you're happy and you know it and you really want to show it
If you're happy and you know it…"

**ELGs for behaviour and self-control
Lesson 2**

Pupils should be taught to:
Begin to accept the needs of others, with support

Resources:
A parcel with as many layers of paper as children, with something in the middle labelled 'To be shared by the group' e.g. a bottle of bubbles, a book.

Introductory phase:
Reflections. The children copy the practitioner's simple actions e.g., brushing teeth, eating breakfast, getting dressed.

Middle phase:
Show the children the parcel and ask who they think should open it?

Is there any way to open it so everyone feels happy?

Suggest to them it is a parcel with many layers of paper so you are going to play pass the parcel. Ensure every child has a turn to take off one layer of paper. At the end of the game, share with the entire group the prize. (If your group is more than 12 it may take too long for every child to take off a layer of paper.)

Explain to the children that by playing the game and sharing the prize, everyone feels happy. How would they have felt if one person opened the parcel and kept the prize?

Closing phase/plenary:
Congratulate the children for thinking of others and playing the game so well.

Clap and touch The children copy the practitioner who gives two claps and touches a part of her body with both hands, (e.g., clap, clap, touch head, clap, clap, touch knees), change the speed of clapping and touching.

ELGs for behaviour and self-control
Lesson 3

Pupils should be taught to:
Show care and concern for others, for living things and the environment

Resources:
A puppet

Introductory phase:
Pass a handshake and a hello The practitioner smiles at one of the children next to her, shakes their hand, and says "Hello," this is passed around the circle until it gets back to the practitioner.

Middle phase:
Introduce the puppet who is feeling sad because someone called him nasty names. What could the children do to cheer him up?

Take some of their suggestions and add to it:
Body band. To the tune of 'Old Macdonald had a farm:
"Your name had a band, E - I - E - I - O,
And in that band she had some claps E - I - E - I - O,
With a clap clap here, and a clap clap there,
Here a clap there a clap, everywhere a clap clap,
Your name had a band E - I - E - I - O."

Add other body sounds, e.g., stamp, click fingers, yawn.

Ask the puppet if he is feeling any happier. He replies he feels really happy and hopes that none of the children in the group will call anyone nasty names.

Closing phase/plenary:
The practitioner and the children stand up and hold hands. They swing their arms and chant 'We are special'.
On the word 'special', (still holding hands), everyone raises their arms above their heads. They then lower their arms and repeat the sentence.

ELGs for behaviour and self-control **Lesson 4**
Pupils should be taught to: Show care and concern for others, for living things and the environment
Resources: A speaking object
Introductory phase: **Name clap** All the children clap twice and then say the name of a child, e.g., clap, clap, Jessica. Continue around the circle until all the children have had a turn at being named. **Round** 'My name is………' Encourage the children to say all their names.
Middle phase: Ask if any of the children have younger brothers or sisters. If so, ask them how they help to care for them. If not talk about how much care babies and toddlers need. Congratulate the children for being so caring. Ask them who in the group is good at caring for others. Tell them about incidents where you have seen them showing care and concern for each other.
Closing phase/plenary: The teacher and the children stand up and hold hands. They swing their arms and chant 'We are special'. On the word 'special,' (still holding hands), everyone raises their arms above their heads. They then lower their arms and repeat the sentence.

ELGs for behaviour and self-control
Lesson 5

Pupils should be taught to:
Show care and concern for others, for living things and the environment

Resources:
A speaking object
An animal puppet or soft toy

Introductory phase:
To the tune of 'Old Macdonald' change the words so that he had a pet and sing various verses mentioning pets,

"Old Macdonald had a farm, E - I - E - I - O,
And on that farm he had a dog E - I - E - I - O,
With a woof, woof here and a woof, woof there,
Here a woof, there a woof, everywhere a woof, woof,
Old Macdonald had a farm, E - I - E - I - O."

Middle phase:
Ask if any of the children have a pet at home and ask how they care for it? If not tell the group about caring for various pets.

If the children could have a pet to care for what would they like to have.
Round   "I would like to have a ..."

Closing phase/plenary:
Remind the children that all living things need care.

Introduce the puppet or soft toy and tell the group that pets, like cats and dogs like to be stroked gently. The children are going to have a chance to say goodbye to the puppet and stroke him very gently. They can say "No" to stroking him.

ELGs for behaviour and self control
Lesson 6

Pupils should be taught to:
Show care and concern for others, for living things and the environment

Resources:
A speaking object

Introductory phase:
Tell the children they are going to play a game where they need to listen.
Body game Using body part names ask the children to perform actions e.g. look at your knees, tap your shoulder with one hand, stand on one leg, blink your eyes, scratch your nose.

Congratulate the children for listening.

Middle phase:
Ask the children to think about the outside places they like to visit or play in. It might be their garden or a park, or on their street, or in the outside area at the setting.
Round "I like to go to..."

Ask them why they chose those places, e.g., it is a lovely place to play and to look at the: sky, grass, trees, flowers, birds, etc.

What can the children do to care for the outside? e.g., not drop litter, don't pick flowers unless an adult says they can, help to plant trees and other plants.

Closing phase/plenary:
Remind the children they have to care for the environment.

Copy a ripple The practitioner wiggles her fingers explaining that she is making rain. The children copy. The practitioner changes the action to thunder, slapping her knees, or wind, waving her arms. The practitioner performs the various movements and ends by bringing out the sun by miming a circle with her hands. Everyone smiles.

ELGs for behaviour and self-control
Lesson 7

Pupils should be taught to:
Understand what is right, what is wrong and why

Resources:
A speaking object
A right and wrong list

Introductory phase:
Copy a ripple   The practitioner wiggles her fingers explaining that she is making rain. She passes this on to the child next to her. That child passes it on to the next, and so on around the circle. When all the children are wiggling their fingers the practitioner changes the action to thunder, slapping her knees, or wind, waving her arms. The practitioner sends various movements around the circle in quick succession and ends by bringing out the sun by miming a circle with her hands. Everyone smiles.

Congratulate the children for doing the right actions.

Middle phase:
This lesson is about knowing about right and wrong actions.
Use the right and wrong sheet, (you can use your own incidents) and ask children to put thumbs up if the action is right and down if the action is wrong.

Ask them to think of one wrong action.
Round "A wrong thing to do is…"

Ask them to think of one right thing they have done recently.
Round "The right thing I did was…"

If they can't think of a right action you can supply them with one and then get them to say it.

Closing phase/plenary:
Ask the children to think about whether what they are doing is a right or a wrong thing to do.

Train game   The children listen and copy the rhythm. Start the chant slowly and gradually build up speed and momentum, like a train pulling away from a platform, until the final "RRIIIIGHT" sounds like the train whistle.
    Listening (x 4)
    Being gentle (x 4)
    Kind and helpful (x 4)
    Working hard (x 4)

    RRIIIIGHT!!!!!!!!

Words can be changed to emphasise any right actions.

Right and wrong list

- Hurting somebody in the playground

- Being gentle

- Interrupting when someone else is talking

- Helping at home

- Taking something that does not belong to you

- Being kind and helpful

- Hitting somebody back if they hit you first

- Caring for a new child in school

- Trying to finish your work at school

- Not telling the truth

ELGs for behaviour and self-control
Lesson 8

Pupils should be taught to:
Understand what is right, what is wrong and why

Resources:
A speaking object
Two puppets

Introductory phase:
123 clap 1 clap means the children stand up, 2 claps mean jump on the spot and 3 claps mean sit down. The practitioner claps and the children try to do the right action. Really make it fun and try to trick the class.

Congratulate the children for doing the right actions.

Middle phase:
This lesson is about knowing about right and wrong actions.

Introduce the puppets Salt and Pepper and act out a scenario of wrong actions. You can use an incident that has happened in your group. Alternatively:

Pepper is playing nicely with her toys when Salt comes and tries to play as well.
Pepper: Go away I don't want you to play, you are too bossy
Salt: Oh go on let me play.

Pepper tries to push Salt away and then they start fighting, both puppets get hurt and cry.

Ask the children what were the wrong things that happened. Not letting some one else play, calling names, pushing, fighting.

What would have been the right thing to do?

Ask if anyone is brave enough to tell about something that they now know they did that was wrong?

Congratulate any child who realises that what they did was wrong, and of course they are now sorry, which means that they will try not do it again.

Ask the children to think about a right thing they did this week.
Round "The right thing I did was…"

Closing phase/plenary:
Ask the children to think about whether what they are doing is a right or a wrong thing to do.

Train game The children listen and copy the rhythm. Start the chant slowly and gradually build up speed and momentum, like a train pulling away from a platform, until the final "RRIIIIGHT" sounds like the train whistle.
        Listening (x 4)
        Being gentle (x 4)
        Kind and helpful (x 4)
        Working hard (x 4)

        RRIIIIGHT!!!!!!!!

Words can be changed to emphasise any right actions.

ELGs for behaviour and self-control
Lesson 9

Pupils should be taught to:
Understand what is right, what is wrong and why

Resources:
A speaking object

Introductory phase:
Labels   Alternately label the children. You could use suitable words from your topic, e.g., cat/dog, red/blue, square/circle or you could use three or four labels e.g. bus/car/lorry/train. The practitioner calls out one of the labels and all the children with that label have to stand up and change seats. It works well if you try to trick them by calling out the same label a few times.

If the children pushed each other during the first playing, ask if they could play it without pushing. Play it again with all the class trying to play it, showing concern for others, not pushing, and not getting too excited.

Did the game feel better when they played it with concern for others?

Middle phase:
This lesson is about knowing the difference between right and wrong actions.

Tell the children they are going to behave like robots. They are machines, they have to do everything you, or a chosen child says:

Stand up, walk around the room, move slowly backwards, dance etc.

Explain that robots have no choice about how they behave, but children do. They know the difference between right and wroing and it is up to them to choose the right behaviour.

Ask the children to think of a right choice.
Round "The right thing I did was…"
If the children can't think of any, help them out by reminding them of the right action they might have done.

Congratulate the children for knowing what is right and wrong.

Closing phase/plenary:
In this game, you have to listen before you know whether to do the action, you do not have a choice.

Simon says   The practitioner or a child gives instructions. If Simon says do it, the children do the action. The children should not do the action if Simon did not say so.

ELGs for behaviour and self-control
Lesson 10

Pupils should be taught to:
Consider the consequences of their words and actions for themselves and others

Resources:
A speaking object

Introductory phase:
Play oranges and lemons to ensure children are mixed up in the circle. The children are alternately labelled "Orange" or "Lemon." The practitioner says either "oranges" or "lemons" and the children change seats with the same fruit. If "Fruit Basket" is called, all the children change seats.

If the children start to push in order to change seats, stop them, and ask them to think about how they are behaving and to try to change places without pushing other children. If they play the game in a gentle manner congratulate them for thinking of others.

Middle phase:
Pass a smile The practitioner smiles at the child on their right, who then passes the smile on around the circle. Encourage eye contact
How do you feel when someone smiles at you?
Round "When someone smiles at me I feel..."

Just by smiling we can make other people feel happy, glad, warm inside, special, etc.

What things do we do that make other people feel cross?
Round "I make others cross when I... "

Closing phase/plenary:
Ask the children during the next week to think about how they are making other people feel.

We are going to finish the lesson by trying to make everyone feel happy.

Pass-a-toe. The children stand up in a circle at first and join hands. They then drop hands. The practitioner says that instead of a smile we are going to pass different parts of our body around the circle. Start with toes; children gently touch the toe of the child next to them in the circle, with their toe. When everyone has had a turn repeat with knees, thumbs, elbows, fingertips, etc. End with a smile followed by a clap for everyone.

ELGs for behaviour and self-control
Lesson 11

Pupils should be taught to:
Consider the consequences of their words and actions for themselves and others

Resources:
A speaking object

Introductory phase:
Aiken Drum Faces Change the words after the chorus

Chorus
> 'There was a man lived in the moon, lived in the moon, lived in the moon,
> There was a man lived in the moon and his name was Aiken Drum.
>
> His face was always… sad, angry, excited, happy etc. (x 3)
> His face was always …sad, etc, and his name was Aiken Drum.

Ask the children to make their faces and voices fit the words in the song, always finish with happy!

Pass a smile The practitioner smiles at the child on their right, who then passes the smile on around the circle. Encourage eye contact.

Middle phase:
Ask the children to think about what else you can do to make others feel happy.
Round "To make people happy I can…"

If you have made someone happy how do you feel?

Some words can make others feel happy, can anyone think of any?
Hello, Thank You, Please, Let's share, You can play, I like you, Can I help? Etc.

What do you like others to say to you?
Round "I like others to say…"

Closing phase/plenary:
Ask the children during the next week to think about how they are making other people feel.

We are going to finish the lesson by trying to make everyone feel happy.

Pass-a-toe. The children stand up in a circle at first and join hands. They then drop hands. The practitioner says that instead of a smile we are going to pass different parts of our body around the circle. Start with toes; children gently touch the toe of the child next to them in the circle, with their toe. When everyone has had a turn repeat with: knees, thumbs, elbows, fingertips, etc. End with a smile followed by a clap for everyone.

ELGs for behaviour and self-control
Lesson 12

Pupils should be taught to:
Consider the consequences of their words and actions for themselves and others

Resources:
A speaking object
Happy mood music

Introductory phase:
Golden River The practitioner is the keeper.

The children chant:

'Keeper keeper may we cross your Golden River?'

The keeper replies, 'Only if you are... (Use positive attributes, e.g., kind, friendly, helpful, gentle). The children change seats with children who have the same attribute.

Middle phase:
Tell the children to think of something they have done that made someone else happy. They are going to mime the action and the rest of the class is going to try to guess what they did. If they find it difficult start off with your own.

How did they feel when they made someone feel happy?
Ask the children to think of something they could do to make someone feel happy
Round "I could...."
They could mime this for the rest of the class.

Closing phase/plenary:
Remind the children that their words and actions affect others and themselves.

Children close their eyes and put their hands on their knees with the palms facing upwards and their fingers slightly curled. This relaxes their shoulders and most children find it easier to sit still in this position. Using a mood music tape encourage children to close their eyes and listen and try and picture themselves doing something that makes them feel happy. Notice any that start to move in time with the music, and explain that music can affect how we feel.

Pass a friendly squeeze. The practitioner squeezes the hand of one of the children sitting next to her, who passes it on to the next child, and so on around the circle until the squeeze is passed back to the practitioner.

Further Activities and Strategies for Behaviour and Self-control

♦ Set, explain, and maintain clear, reasonable and consistent limits.

♦ Share the policy for behaviour management with parents.

♦ Model appropriate behaviour showing care and concern for all.

♦ Affirm and praise appropriate behaviour.

♦ Use adjacent praise, so that children are aware of the appropriate way to behave.

♦ Display pictorial examples of children behaving appropriately.

♦ Listen to children when they raise injustices and involve them in resolving conflicts.

♦ Choose appropriate stories and poems.

♦ Reward appropriate behaviour.

♦ Provide children with opportunities to handle living things.

♦ Organise a 'bring a pet day' so that all children are aware of the needs of pets.

♦ Grow plants.

♦ Talk about the environment and how people look after it.

♦ Encourage children to keep the setting and other areas tidy and litter free.

ELGs for self – care and health and bodily awareness
Lesson 1

Pupils should be taught to:
Demonstrate a sense of pride in their own achievement

Resources:
None

Introductory phase:
Animal game – The practitioner goes around the circle telling each child they are one of three animals, e.g. duck, cow or dog. When their animal is mentioned the children make appropriate noises. When 'farmyard' is said all the animals make their noise.

Middle phase:
Tell the children you are going to sing a song about some of the things that they can do.

Sing the chorus of 'Here we go round the Mulberry Bush'.

After the chorus sing verses about things the group can do e.g. wash our hands, eat our dinner, go to sleep, go for a walk.

Include actions and ask the group for suggestions of things they can do.

Closing phase/plenary:
Congratulate the group for being able to do so many things.

The practitioner and the children stand up and hold hands. They swing their arms and chant 'We are special'. On the word 'special', (still holding hands) everyone raises their arms above their heads; they then lower their arms and repeat the sentence.

ELGs for self–care and health and bodily awareness
Lesson 2

Pupils should be taught to:
Demonstrate a sense of pride in their own achievement

Resources:
A speaking object
A puppet
Some music for musical statues

Introductory phase:
Tell the children you are going to sing a song about some of the things that they can do.
Sing the chorus of
    'Here we go round the Mulberry Bush'.

After the chorus sing verses about things the group can do e.g. wash our hands, eat our dinner, go to sleep, go for a walk.

Include actions and ask the group for suggestions of things they can do.

Middle phase:
Introduce the puppet Salt who tells the children some of the things he can do e.g.,
Salt: Hello children I can clean my teeth. Put your thumb up if you can

Salt: I can put my shoes on. Put your thumb up if you can.

Salt: I can hop on one foot. Put your thumb up if you can.

Salt: I can build with Lego. Put your thumb up if you can.

Salt: I can wash my hands. Put your thumb up if you can.

Ask the children to think about the things they can do.
Round   "I can…"
If any child cannot think of anything, help them.

Closing phase/plenary:
Musical statues with mime   The children stand and the practitioner gives them a task to do, e.g., cleaning their teeth, whilst the music is played. When the music stops they must freeze. Anyone who moves is out and sits down.

Congratulate the group for being able to do so many things.

ELGs for self–care and health and bodily awareness
Lesson 3

Pupils should be taught to:
Show an awareness of healthy practices with regard to eating, sleeping and hygiene

Resources:
A speaking object
Pictures of healthy food or the real thing, including fruit, vegetables, fish, meat, bread, cereals, dairy products

Introductory phase:
We all belong to this group and we are going to sing our group band song,
Body band to the tune of 'Old Macdonald had a farm.
"Your name had a band, E - I - E - I - O,
And in that band she had some claps E - I - E - I - O,
With a clap clap here, and a clap clap there,
Here a clap, there a clap, everywhere a clap clap,
Your name had a band E - I - E - I - O."

Add other body sounds, e.g., stamp, click fingers, yawn.

Congratulate the children for using their bodies to create a band.

Middle phase:
Ask if anyone knows what keeping healthy means. It means feeling well and happy
We need to keep our bodies healthy. Does anyone know what we need to do to keep healthy?

Explain that one thing we need to do is to eat different healthy food. Show the pictures and ask the children to put their thumbs up if they eat that food.

Tell the group to think about their favourite food.
Round "I like to eat… "

Closing phase/plenary:
To stay healthy we need to eat different types of food and we need to drink.

Clap and touch The children copy the practitioner who gives two claps and touches a part of her body with both hands, (e.g., clap, clap, touch head, clap, clap, touch knees). Change the speed of clapping and touching.

ELGs for self–care and health and bodily awareness
Lesson 4

Pupils should be taught to:
Show an awareness of healthy practices with regard to eating, sleeping and hygiene

Resources:
A speaking object
Pictures of food and drink, some healthy, some less healthy
2 different coloured hoops

Introductory phase:
Mime pass Pretend to wash and dry hands then mime passing food around the circle, e.g., ice cream cone, a bag of hot chips, a bowl of jelly, a cup of water, a large juicy apple.

Middle phase:
Explain that this lesson we are thinking about which food we can eat a lot of because it helps to keep us healthy, and which food we should eat a little of, because it is sugary or fatty, so that it will be eaten as a treat.

Using the pictures or real food, ask the children to help you to put the food into the hoops. One hoop is for food that you can eat as much of as you like, and the other hoop is for treats or things that you shouldn't eat or drink too much of, because of sugar or fat content.

Ask them to think of one food or drink that is in the healthy hoop that they like.
Round "I like…"

Closing phase/plenary:
To stay healthy we need to eat different types of food and we need to drink plenty of liquid.

Train game The children listen and copy the rhythm. Start the chant slowly and gradually build up speed and momentum, like a train pulling away from a station platform, until the final "fruit" sounds like the train whistle.

　　Cup of water (x 4)
　　Green beans (x 4)
　　Brown bread (x 4)
　　Sandwiches　(x 4)
　　FRUUIIIITTT

Words can be changed to include any healthy food or drink.

ELGs for self–care and health and bodily awareness
Lesson 5

Pupils should be taught to:
Show an awareness of healthy practices with regard to eating, sleeping and hygiene

Resources:
A speaking object
A puppet
Three different percussion instruments

Introductory phase:
Percussion actions - The practitioner uses the different instrument to tell the children what to do. E.g. drum, stand up, and march; shaker, shake all over; bell, clap hands together. When children become proficient hide the instruments, so that they cannot see what is being played.

Middle phase:
Introduce the puppet who says he is not feeling very well. He tells the children he is feeling tired and grumpy. Ask the children to put their thumbs up if they ever feel tired and grumpy?

What makes them feel like that?
It is usually because they have not had enough sleep.
Ask if anyone finds it hard to go to sleep?

Ask them to think about what helps them to go to sleep. It might be having a story read to them, having a light left on, having a goodnight kiss from Mum/Dad/Carer, having a cup of milk before they go to bed.
Round "I go to sleep after…"

Closing phase/plenary:
Explain that to stay healthy we need to eat different types of food, we need to drink, and we need to have enough sleep.

Mime The practitioner mimes getting ready for bed using some of the children's suggestions from the previous round. The children copy the mime.

ELGs for self–care and health and bodily awareness
Lesson 6

Pupils should be taught to:
Show an awareness of healthy practices with regard to eating, sleeping and hygiene

Resources:
A speaking object

Introductory phase:
Clap and touch. The children copy the practitioner. The adult who gives two claps and touches a part of her body with both hands, (e.g., clap, clap, head, clap, clap, touch knees). Change the speed of clapping and touching.

Middle phase:
Tell the children we are going to sing about all the things we do to keep clean and healthy e.g., wash our hands, clean our teeth, have a bath/shower, wash our hair to the tune of 'Here we go round the Mulberry Bush.'

Ask children to think about when they wash their hands.
Round "I wash my hands …"

Mime washing and drying hands and stress how important it is to wash hands after going to the lavatory and before eating or drinking.

Closing phase/plenary:
Explain that to stay healthy we need to eat different types of food, we need to drink, we need to have enough sleep, and we need to be clean, especially our hands.

To end the lesson we are going to use our hands to:

Copy a ripple The practitioner wiggles her fingers explaining that she is making rain. The children copy. The practitioner changes the action to thunder – slapping her knees, or wind, waving her arms. The practitioner performs the various movements and ends by bringing out the sun by miming a circle with her hands. Everyone smiles.

ELGs for self–care and health and bodily awareness
Lesson 7

Pupils should be taught to:
Dress and undress independently

Resources:
A speaking object
A selection of appropriate clothing e.g. hats, gloves, coats, scarves, shoes, wellingtons
Some music and a bean bag

Introductory phase:
Body band to the tune of 'Old Macdonald had a farm.
    "Your name had a band, E - I - E - I - O,
    And in that band she had some claps E – I – E – I – O,
    With a clap clap here, and a clap clap there,
    Here a clap, there a clap, everywhere a clap clap,
    Your name had a band E –I – E –I –O."

Add other body sounds, e.g., stamp, click fingers, yawn.

Middle phase:
Explain that our bodies need clothes. Ask what sort of clothes the children wear in the winter..
Round "In the winter I wear…."

What about in the summer when it is really warm?
Round "In the summer I wear…."
Ask why it is important to wear a hat when the sun is shining?

Tell the children they are going to play a game. They are going to pass the beanbag around the circle and when the music stops the child holding the beanbag has to go into the middle of the circle and put on the clothes that you say. In this way, you can make the item appropriate to the child.

Ask the children to think about which item of clothing they find most difficult to put on or take off.
Round "The hardest thing to put on or off is…"

Closing phase/plenary:
Tell the children that practice is the way to get better at something, so they should practise putting on the clothes that they find difficult.

Pass a smile The practitioner smiles at the child on their right, who then passes the smile on around the circle. Encourage eye contact.

ELGs for self–care and health and bodily awareness
Lesson 8

Pupils should be taught to:
Manage their own personal hygiene

Resources:
A speaking object

Introductory phase:
Guess who – Three or four children stand in the middle of the circle. The rest of the children close their eyes and the practitioner touches one of the children in the middle who then makes an animal noise e.g. 'quack quack'. The children in the circle try to guess which child made the noise. This can be repeated changing the children in the middle of the circle.

Middle phase:
Ask the children why is it important to wash their hands after a visit to the lavatory?

Ask them to demonstrate washing and drying their hands. What else is it important to do when you visit the lavatory? e.g. flush.

Ask when do you wash your hands besides after using the lavatory
Round "I wash my hands…"

Tell the class you are going to say some good and some bad things to do with keeping clean. If they think it is a good idea they should put their thumb up and smile, if it's a bad idea they put their thumb down and look very sad:

> Peter cleans his teeth every morning, Alan wipes his nose on his sleeve, Jean never washes her hands after she has been to the toilet, Jack washes his hands before he eats his dinner, Jessica has a bath everyday. (You and the children can add to this list.)

If you wash your hands when you have been to the lavatory and before you eat your food you will help to keep your body fit and healthy.

What does it mean to be fit and healthy?

It means feeling well and happy.

Closing phase/plenary:
Remind children how important it is to keep their hands clean.

Mime pass – Food is going to be passed around the circle, so children must mime washing their hands. Then mime passing jelly, cup of tea, ice-cream, toast, etc.

ELGs for self–care and health and bodily awareness
Lesson 9

Pupils should be taught to:
Manage their own personal hygiene

Resources:
A speaking object

Introductory phase:
Tell the children you are going to sing a song about some of the things that they can do to keep clean and healthy.

Sing the chorus of 'Here we go round the Mulberry Bush'. After the chorus sing verses about things the group can do, e.g., wash our hands, clean our teeth, have a bath, and use a hanky.

Middle phase:
Ask them to feel their teeth with their tongues. Can they feel the different types of teeth? Why is it important that they clean their teeth?

Explain they will lose one set of teeth to make room for their strong adult ones, but even so, they need to take care of their milk teeth.

Ask What do you think is bad for your teeth? (foods and drink that contain sugar.) "What do you think is good for your teeth?" (fruit, milk, brushing them, going to the dentist.)

Round "To care for my teeth I…."

Ask the children to demonstrate cleaning their teeth

Tell them that when they have a cold or a cough it means they have germs in their body so if they sneeze or cough they should use a hanky or a tissue to catch the germs and stop them spreading to others.

Closing phase/plenary:
Round "To stay clean and healthy I…."

Pass–a–toe The children stand up in a circle at first and join hands. Then they drop hands and instead of a smile, pass different parts of their bodies around the circle. Start with toes then knees, thumbs, elbows, fingertips etc.   End with a smile.

**ELGs for behaviour and self–care and health and bodily awareness
Lesson 10**

Pupils should be taught to:
Recognise the importance of keeping healthy and those things which contribute to this.

Resources:
A speaking object
'Balance of good health' – plate showing proportions of food that make up a well-balanced and healthy diet, available from local Health Promotion Units.

Introductory phase:
Play oranges and lemons to ensure the children are mixed up in the circle. The children are alternately labelled "Orange" or "Lemon." The practitioner says either "oranges" or "lemons" and the children change seats with the same fruit. If "Fruit Basket" is called, all the children change seats.

Ask which other fruits the children like to eat?
Round "The fruit I like to eat is…"

Middle phase:
Explain that fruit is one food that helps to keep us healthy.

Think about what else you eat to stay healthy
Round "To stay healthy I eat…"

Explain it is important to eat different things. We have talked about fruit. Vegetables are also good for you. Which vegetables do you like?
Round "I like to eat…"

Explain that bread, cereals, and potatoes are good for us too. Put your thumbs up if you like bread, potatoes, cereal.

Tell children they should also try to eat some meat or fish, beans, milk, cheese, yoghurt.

The things we should eat less of are foods with sugar, like sweets, and food with fat, like chips or crisps. Which of those foods full of sugar or fat would you chose for a treat?
Round "For a treat I would chose …"

Closing phase/plenary:
If you have a copy of the 'Balance of good health' show it to the class.

Children copy you miming eating various foods, ending with a treat.

ELGs for self–care and health and bodily awareness
Lesson 11

Pupils should be taught to:
Recognise the importance of keeping healthy and those things which contribute to this

Resources:
A speaking object

Introductory phase:
Golden River The practitioner is the keeper. The children chant 'Keeper keeper may we cross your Golden River?' The keeper replies, "Only if you can..." (Use physical activities e.g., hop, swim, run, skip,). The children change seats with children who can do the same activity.

Middle phase:
Explain that exercise like jumping, skipping, swimming is important to help us to keep healthy and fit. However, before you do exercise you should warm your body up.

The children copy. Gently move fingers and wrists, move necks, shoulders, and elbows. Stand up and move from the waist, gently exercise knees, ankles, move toes inside your shoes. Be aware of children with a disability.

Congratulate the children for moving their bodies so gently and with control.

Ask them to think about which exercise they like to do to keep healthy
Round "To keep healthy I ..."

Tell the class that sleep is another thing you need to stay healthy. Is there anyone who finds it hard to go to sleep?
If there is ask the other children for tips on how to get to sleep, e.g., having a bedtime story, a cup of warm milk, having the light left on etc.

Closing phase/plenary:
Congratulate the children for knowing so much about keeping healthy.

Train game The children listen and copy the rhythm. Start the chant slowly and gradually build up speed and momentum, like a train pulling away from a station platform, until the final '**sleep**' sounds like the train whistle.

Keep clean, (x 4)
Use a hankie, (x 4)
Food and drink, (x 4)
Exercise, (x 4)
SLEEEEEEP!

ELGs for self – care and health and bodily awareness
Lesson 12

Pupils should be taught to:
Recognise the importance of keeping healthy and those things which contribute to this

Resources:
A speaking object
A rain stick or mood music

Introductory phase:
Simon says   Use body part names in the game, e.g., "Simon says look at your knees, Simon says tap your shoulder with one hand."

Middle phase:
Explain that to keep healthy you need to eat a variety of food, drink, have plenty of exercise and sleep.

You also need to keep yourself safe. Safe means not being scared or hurting yourself or feeling unhappy. Where do you think you have to be careful to keep safe and happy?

Round "I have to be careful..."   (road, park, pool, sea, sun, kitchen etc.)
Follow up what the class tells you and discuss ways of keeping safe in different places.

Sometimes children need to say "No" if something makes them feel scared or unhappy.
Ask what they would say No to.
Round "I would say No..."   You may have to start this round.

Tell the class to think about things they would say Yes to.
Round   "I would say Yes to..."

Closing phase/plenary:
Congratulate the children for knowing so much about keeping healthy and safe.

The children close their eyes and put their hands on their knees with the palms facing upwards and their fingers slightly curled. This relaxes their shoulders and most children find it easier to sit very still in this position. Using a mood music tape or a rain stick, encourage the children to close their eyes and listen, picturing themselves playing on a park, playground or garden. They are feeling happy and safe. After a couple of minutes ask if anyone will share their picture with the class.

Further activities and strategies for self-care and for health and bodily awareness

♦ Give positive feedback.

♦ Provide toys with different fasteners for the children to practise with.

♦ Provide dressing up clothes with various fastenings.

♦ Provide time for the children to put their own clothes on and off.

♦ Play games that encourage the children to dress and undress.

♦ Encourage the children to help each other.

♦ Ensure easily accessed facilities in the lavatories.

♦ Teach basic hygiene skills, and provide appropriate resources.

♦ Model washing hands before touching food etc.

♦ Arrange visits from the dental hygienist, nurse etc.

♦ Ensure that children drink enough water during the day.

♦ Provide healthy snacks.

♦ Ensure that resources are appropriately stored with templates or labels for easy returning.

ELGs for sense of community
Lesson 1

Pupils should be taught to:
Make connections between different parts of their life experience

Resources:
A speaking object
A puppet

Introductory phase:
A musical hello, using the traditional rhyme
   Tommy Thumb, Tommy Thumb Where are you?
Substitute the first two words with:
   'Hello (........), Hello (.........) Where are you?'
The child replies:
   'Here I am, Here I am'
To which you respond:
   'How do you do!'
Smile at each child, try to engage eye contact, and perhaps a handshake.
Continue around in the circle until all the children have had a turn.

Middle phase:
Introduce the puppet.

Salt: 'Hello children. My name is Salt. At home I have a bath, and I watch
         the television, and I play in my garden. What do you do at home?'

Ask the children to think about something that they do at home, that they could tell the
puppet and the rest of the group.

Round "At home I..."

Thank the children for sharing what they do at home with everyone.

Closing phase/plenary:
Clap and touch The children copy the practitioner. The practitioner who gives two claps
and touches a part of her body with both hands (e.g. clap, clap, touch head, clap, clap,
touch knees). Change the speed of the clapping and touching.

ELGs for sense of community
Lesson 2

Pupils should be taught to:
Make connections between different parts of their life experience

Resources:
A speaking object
A puppet

Introductory phase:
Mime pass Mime passing things around the circle that the children would find at home, e.g., a kitten, a baby brother, a favourite toy. Ask the group for other ideas.

Middle phase:
Introduce the puppet.

Salt:　　'Hello children. My name is Salt. At home I like to play in my garden, I like to read my books and play on my computer. What do you like to do at home?'

Ask the children to think about one thing that they like to do at home that they could tell the puppet and the rest of the group.
Round　"At home I like to…"

Thank the children for sharing what they like to do at home with everyone.

Closing phase/plenary:
Congratulate the children for joining in and speaking in the circle.

A musical goodbye – using the traditional rhyme, 'Twinkle twinkle little star'

Sing to each child:
　　'Now it's time to say goodbye (child's name), (child's name), wave goodbye'.

Encourage the children to wave goodbye when their name is sung.

Congratulate the children for doing so well.

ELGs for sense of community
Lesson 3

Pupils should be taught to:
Make connections between different parts of their life experience

Resources:
A speaking object
A puppet
Some music for musical statues

Introductory phase:
Mime simple actions for the children to follow, identifying areas of the body they are touching, e.g., scratch your ear, touch your toes, rub your elbow, click your fingers, blink your eyes.

Follow with lots of praise about how well they did.

Middle phase:
Introduce the puppet.

Salt: 'Hello children my name is Salt. Before I came to the group today I had my breakfast, and I played with my car and I cleaned my teeth.'

Ask the children to think about one thing they did before they came to the group that they could tell Salt and the other children.
Round "One thing I did was…"
If the children want to elaborate, they can as long as the pace of the lesson is not lost.

Thank the children for sharing.

Closing phase/plenary:
Congratulate the children for joining in and speaking in the circle and for listening when other children were speaking.

Tell the children they are going to play a game and they have to listen. They can dance/move to the music but when it stops, they have to stop very still.

ELGs for sense of community
Lesson 4

Pupils should be taught to:
Show a strong sense of self as a member of different communities such as family or setting

Resources:
None

Introductory phase:
Give-a-smile – The practitioner asks the children to look sad. The practitioner smiles, then takes the smile from their face, and gives it to the next child. That child smiles and passes the smile on until everyone is smiling.

Middle phase:
Sing the 'Belonging Song' – to the tune of 'The wheels on the bus.'

   Children in this class/group like to play, like to play, like to play.
   Children in this class/group like to play, all day long.

Add verses that mention children by name and let the child choose their own activity, e.g., Jill in this class likes to skip, Leon in this class likes to paint. Involve as many individual children as possible. Actions can be added.

Ask the children how many of them like to do the activities mentioned in the song. Call the activities out one at a time and children put their thumbs up if they do.

Closing phase/plenary:
Congratulate the children for joining in with the group.

Pass a smile. The practitioner smiles at the child on their right, who then passes the smile on around the circle.

ELGs for sense of community **Lesson 5**
Pupils should be taught to: Show a strong sense of self as a member of different communities such as family or setting
Resources: A speaking object A puppet
Introductory phase: **Catch a smile** All the children and the practitioner stand up. The practitioner makes eye contact with a child and then smiles. The smiled at child smiles and sits down. Continue until everyone has had a turn.
Middle phase: Introduce the puppet. Salt: 'Hello my name is Salt. I live with my Mum and my Gran and my sister.' Ask the children to think about who they live with **Round**   "I live with…" The people they live with are their family. What sort of things do they do with their family at home? e.g., they might watch television together, or read books. **Round** "With my family I…..."
Closing phase/plenary: Thank the children for sharing what they do at home with their family. Be sensitive to children who may not live in a traditional family. **Simon says** Use body part names in the game, e.g., "Simon says look at your knees", "Simon says tap your shoulder with one hand." Children should not do the action if Simon didn't say. Congratulate the children for listening.

ELGs for sense of community
Lesson 6

Learning objective:
To show a strong sense of self as a member of different communities such as family or setting

Resources:
A speaking object
A puppet
Three different percussion instruments

Introductory phase:
Percussion actions – The practitioner uses the different instrument to tell the children what to do. E.g. drum, stand up, and march; shaker, shake all over; bell, clap hands together. When children become proficient hide the instruments, so that they cannot see what is being played.

Middle phase:
Introduce the puppet.

Salt   'Hello my name is Salt. I live with other people in my family. None of us lives alone, but our families or the people we live with are different. With my family I go to the shops, I play in the park' and visit friends.

Ask the children to think about what they do with their family/carers when they go out.
Round   "With my family I…"

Closing phase/plenary:
Thank the children for sharing what they do at home with their family; be sensitive to the different types of families.

Mime pass – using objects from the setting: e.g. water container, bucket of sand, paint brush full of paint.

Silent pass – try to pass the shaker around the circle without it making a noise.

Congratulate the children for working so well together as a group.

ELGs for sense of community
Lesson 7

Pupils should be taught to:
Have a positive self imagine and show that they are comfortable with themselves

Resources:
A speaking object
A small box with a lid and a mirror stuck on the bottom
A rain stick or mood music

Introductory phase:
Belonging Song, to the tune of 'The wheels on the bus'
    Children in this class/group like to play, like to play, like to play.
    Children in this class/group like to play, all day long.

Add verses that mention children by name and let the child choose their own activity, e.g., Jill in this class likes to skip, Leon in this class likes to paint. Involve as many individual children as possible. Actions can be added.

Middle phase:
Tell the children that they are all going to have a turn to look into a special box. In the box they will see someone who is special. They must keep quiet when they have looked and not tell anyone who the special person is. When all the children have had a turn the practitioner asks who the special person was. The children reply "ME"

Explain that this lesson is all about why each person is special. Everybody is to have a good look at everyone else because we are going to say three things that are special about everybody in the class.

The 'special ' child holds the speaking object, which is passed, around the circle, until every child has been 'special'. The rest of the group indicates with their thumb that they know something special about the special child.

If the group are struggling to find things to say the adult in the circle helps them.

Closing phase/plenary:
The practitioner and the children stand up and hold hands. They swing their arms and chant 'We are special'. On the word 'special', they all still holding hands, raise their arms above their heads, they then lower their arms and repeat the sentence.

Explain that you are going to give the children time to think about how special they are. Children close their eyes and put their hands on their knees with the palms facing upwards and their fingers slightly curled. This relaxes their shoulders and most children find it easier to sit very still in this position. Using a rain stick or a mood music tape allow the children to think about what makes them special.

ELGs for sense of community
Lesson 8

Pupils should be taught to:
Have a positive self imagine and show that they are comfortable with themselves

Resources:
A speaking object
Ask the children to bring in something from home that is special to them. You may have to send a note home for this.

Introductory phase:
Mime pass - pass objects around the circle, e.g. an enormous parcel, a puppy, a ladybird.

Middle phase:
Explain that we are all special. You are all different, you look different from each other, you have different things at home, and you like to do different things. You have all brought different special objects from home.

Using the speaking object go around the circle encouraging each child to say two or three sentences about their special artefact.

Thank the children for sharing their special object with the rest of the group.

Closing phase/plenary:
Explain that the children are all different but special. The practitioner and the children stand up and hold hands. They swing their arms and chant 'We are special'. On the word 'special', they all still holding hands, raise their arms above their heads; they then lower their arms and repeat the sentence.

Pass–a–toe The children stand up in a circle. At first join hands, then drop hands and say instead of a smile we are going to pass different parts of our body around the circle. Start with toes, then knees, thumbs, elbows, fingertips etc. End with a smile followed by a clap for everyone.

ELGs for sense of community
Lesson 9

Pupils should be taught to:
Understand that people have different needs, views, cultures and beliefs which need to be treated with respect
Understand that they can expect others to treat their needs, views, cultures and beliefs with respect

Resources:
A speaking object
Ask the children to find out where they were born. You may have to send a note home for this information.
Pictures of children from different ethnic groups

Introductory phase:
Who are we? One child says her name and points to another child, who stands up and repeats the process until all the children are standing.

Middle phase:
Explain that this lesson we are thinking about some of the differences between people.
Ask where were you born?
Round "I was born…"
Show the pictures of children from different ethnic groups.

Ask who can see differences in the children in the circle and the pictures? Concentrate on physical differences, skin, eye, hair colour.

All change Using physical differences. The children change seats, i.e. all children with blue eyes change seats, brown eyes, green/grey eyes, blond hair, brown hair, black hair, fair hair.

Explain that it does not matter what you look like. It is what you are like and how you behave that is important.

All change This time the children change seats using positive behaviour criteria; they can listen, are kind, play nicely, care, are happy, are gentle, are helpful. Add your own ideas to the list.

Closing phase/plenary:
Explain that although we are all different, we all need to feel loved and cared for. We should try to respect the differences between people, that means treating each other with kindness and consideration.

Catch a smile All the children and the practitioner stand up. The practitioner makes eye contact with a child and then smiles. The smiled at child smiles and sits down. Continue until everyone has had a turn.

ELGs for sense of community **Lesson 10**

Pupils should be taught to:
Understand that people have different needs, views, cultures and beliefs which need to be treated with respect
Understand that they can expect others to treat their needs, views, cultures and beliefs with respect

Resources:
A speaking object
Some multicultural recipe books or pictures of multicultural food or multicultural food

Introductory phase:
Golden River One child is chosen to be the keeper. The other children chant 'Keeper keeper may we cross your Golden River?' The keeper replies, only if you are …(e.g., wearing a watch, have brown eyes, had breakfast). Any children who fit into the chosen category stand up and swap seats. The keeper tries to catch one of them who then becomes the keeper.

Middle phase:
This lesson we are thinking about some of the differences between people. We are going to concentrate on the different food we like to eat.

Using the pictures or the real food, ask children to put their thumbs up if they have tried the various dishes. It is important to offer a wide variety.

Ask the children to think about one thing they don't like to eat.
Round "One thing I don't like to eat is… "

Now think of your favourite food.
Round "My favourite food is…"

Closing phase/plenary:
Explain that we are all different but in some ways, we are the same. We all eat food although we like different sorts. We should try to respect the differences between people that means treating each other with kindness and consideration.

Train game. The children listen and copy the rhythm. Start the chant slowly and gradually build up speed and momentum, like a train pulling away from a station platform, until the final "noodles" sounds like the train whistle.

    Cup of water, (x 4)
    Beef curry, (x 4)
    Fish and chips, (x 4)
    Fried rice, (x 4)
    NNNOOOODDLLLES!

Words can be changed to fit in with the food mentioned in your lesson.

ELGs for sense of community
Lesson 11

Pupils should be taught to:
Understand that people have different needs, views, cultures and beliefs which need to be treated with respect
Understand that they can expect others to treat their needs, views, cultures and beliefs with respect

Resources:
A speaking object
Artefacts/objects from different beliefs
A rain stick or mood music

Introductory phase:
Golden River   One child is chosen to be the keeper. The other children chant 'Keeper keeper may we cross your Golden River?' The keeper replies, only if you are …(e.g., wearing a watch, have brown eyes, had breakfast.) Any children who fit into the chosen category stand up and swap seats. The keeper tries to catch one of them who then becomes the keeper.

Explain that in the game the children change seats when they have something in common with others. Now we are thinking about the differences between people.

Middle phase:
Show the artefacts and ask if anyone knows what they are and what they are used for? If the children in the class do not know about the artefacts, explain that different religions have different beliefs and different artefacts. Your objects could include: Jewish; Kippah, Menorah, Christian; Bible or Cross, Hinduism; Diva lamps, Conch shells.

Also explain about some of the different festivals or celebrations, e.g., Jewish (Passover), Christian (Christmas), Muslim (Ramadan), Hindu (Divali).

Ask the children if they celebrate any of the festivals? If so what do they do?

Round "The best thing we do when we celebrate is……"

Closing phase/plenary:
Explain we are all different but we should respect the differences between people, that means treating each other with kindness and consideration.
Round "The kind thing I did was…."

The practitioner and the children stand up and hold hands. They swing their arms and chant 'We are special'. On the word 'special', they all still holding hands, raise their arms above their heads, they then lower their arms and repeat the sentence.

Explain that you are going to give the children time to think about how special they are. Children close their eyes and put their hands on their knees with the palms facing upwards and their fingers slightly curled. This relaxes their shoulders and most children find it easier to sit very still in this position. Using a rain stick or a mood music tape allow the children to think about what makes them special.

ELGs for sense of community
Lesson 12

Pupils should be taught to:
Understand that people have different needs, views, cultures and beliefs which need to be treated with respect
Understand that they can expect others to treat their needs, views, cultures and beliefs with respect

Resources:
A speaking object
Some music representing different ethnic groups

Introductory phase:
Using the music from different cultures play musical statues.

Middle phase:
Explain that we have just heard music from different ethnic groups but this lesson we are thinking about what is the same about everyone.

Explain that we have different coloured hair, skin, and eyes but we are all very much alike.

Ask the children to think about what things we have in common. Think about your bodies.
Round "We all have… (eyes, nose, mouth, etc.)

Ask the children to think about things that all people need; whatever the colour of their skin, or wherever they live or whatever they believe.
Round "We all need…" Food, drink, sleep, exercise, love, care, to be healthy, to learn.

Closing phase/plenary:
Explain we are all different in some ways but we are the same in others. We all need treating with kindness and consideration.

Pass a friendly squeeze The practitioner squeezes the hand of one of the children sitting next to her, who passes it on to the next child, and so on around the circle, until the squeeze is passed back to the practitioner.

We have eyes, noses, mouths...

Further activities and strategies for a sense of community

◆ Arrange cultural events involving adults from the community as positive role models.

◆ Invite family members and members of the community to the setting.

◆ Introduce appropriate resources into role-play.

◆ Introduce different ethnic groups through books and displays.

◆ Encourage children to bring in artefacts/objects from home to show to the group.

◆ Organise displays about different ethnic groups.

◆ Taste food from different countries.

◆ Appropriate stories.

◆ Use materials that are accurate and non-stereotypical.

◆ Celebrate festivals from different ethnic groups.

◆ Celebrate special events e.g. weddings, christenings.

Books and other resources

Turn Your School Round by Jenny Mosley (LDA)

Best-selling management manual giving a clear picture of the Quality Circle Time approach, emphasising the need for it to be a whole school policy and including guidelines and practical examples for a range of situations.

Quality Circle Time in the Primary School by Jenny Mosley (LDA)

Invaluable guide to getting started and building strategies to promote self-esteem and positive behaviour, for teachers wishing to put the Whole School Quality Circle Time model into their classrooms, with hundreds of ideas and lesson plans.

More Quality Circle Time by Jenny Mosley (LDA)

Sequel to the above enabling you to evaluate and enhance your current Circle Time practice, raising it to even more exciting and creative levels. Includes ten-minute circle times for nursery children to practise specific skills.

Photocopiable Materials for use with the Jenny Mosley Circle Time Model by Jenny Mosley (Positive Press)

Make life easier with a wealth of charts, target sheets, achievement ladders, awards, congratulations cards, invitations and much more, including tips to help you quickly put them to good use.

All Round Success by Jenny Mosley (Wiltshire County Council)

Simply set-out practical ideas and games for circle time, tried and tested in a year-long project with primary teachers.

Coming Round Again by Jenny Mosley (Wiltshire County Council)

Following on from the above, pulling together a range of fun activities that provide excellent learning opportunities for PSHE and citizenship themes. Explains the rationale behind Circle Time and includes problem-solving ideas.

Circle Time (Positive Press)

User-friendly booklet built around Jenny Mosley's whole school approach, with practical lesson plans for KS1 and KS2 based on an original project in Belfast and now updated.

The Circle Book by Jenny Mosley (Positive Press)

A booklet of feedback and comments (by children and adults) originally compiled in response to the Elton Report (1989) and building on research study results. Updated with more ideas for activities.

Working Towards a Whole School Policy on Self-Esteem and Positive Behaviour by Jenny Mosley (Positive Press)

A booklet of guidelines for operating an effective policy involving teachers, MDSAs, parents, governors and children.

Guidelines for Primary Midday Supervisors by Jenny Mosley (Wiltshire County Council)

A friendly self-help booklet for lunchtime supervisors to use in developing skills in their role as positive models for the children, supporting your school in the creation of secure and happy playtimes.

Create Happier Lunchtimes by Jenny Mosley (Wiltshire County Council)

Sequel to the above, reminding lunchtime supervisors of the importance of their role, offering extra ideas and both indoor and outdoor games.

Assemblies to Teach Golden Rules by Margaret Goldthorpe and Lucy Nutt (LDA)

Ideal if your assemblies could use more 'pep'! Scripts and ideas for creative, fun presentations themed on the moral values behind Golden Rules, based on positive reward for good behaviour rather than punishment for negative actions.

Poems for Circle Time and Literacy hour by Margaret Goldthorpe (LDA)

A much loved book by one of Jenny's senior consultants. Poems of simplicity and fun introduce children in a relaxed way to serious issues such as bullying and can then provide the theme for circle time.

Training video: Quality Circle Time in Action (LDA)

Introduced and performed by Jenny Mosley and ideal for staff training, this video demonstrates the model in use with unrehearsed KS1 and KS2 children. The phases and their rationale are explained by Jenny using many of the resources listed here for sale. With accompanying handbook.

Jenny Mosley's Self-Esteem Builders Kit

Set of colourful high-quality resources to get your school quickly started with Quality Circle Time. Contains motivational stickers for congratulating children on moral values and circle time skills; two colourful themed class target sheets with reusable stickers to mark progress in positive behaviour; reward certificates for achievements such as deciding to improve; responsibility badges for boosting children's self-esteem through special tasks; and a golden rules poster set for classroom and playground. Items also available separately.

Jenny Mosley's Quality Circle Time Kitbag

Costume and treasures to inspire creative circle times: contains 'magic' cloak, blindfold, hand-painted egg (for use as talking object), South American rainstick, small teddy bear, two charming hand puppets and 'treasure chest', together with cassette tape and booklet of lesson ideas. Rainstick, eggs and puppets also available separately.

Playground Friends Baseball Cap

Brightly coloured incentive to support your whole school lunchtime policy, which advocates choosing pupil helpers to befriend marginalised or bewildered children. A 'badge of office' to be worn with pride. Friendship Stops for children seeking help also in preparation.

Here We Go Round by Jenny Mosley and Helen Sonnet.

Written for the Early Years classroom of 3 – 5 year old children in response to the DfES's Early Learning Goals, this book will be indispensable. Following the Quality Circle Time rationale, there are activity plans for ten circle sessions for each of the six areas of learning, with guidance notes, objectives and fun ideas to continue the themes. Well planned and carefully age-appropriate, here is an exciting formula to develop listening, confidence, thinking and spoken language skills.

Ring of Confidence by Penny Vine and Teresa Todd

'The Ring of Confidence programme offers sensitive guidelines and 13 clear lesson plans for the Foundation Stage for practitioners working with under 5's to tackle the vexed issue of Child Protection and substance abuse...it advocates involvement of parents to support and endorse the key issues provided by this thoughtful and user-friendly programme.

For further details and to order contact:

Jenny Mosley Consultancies / Positive Press Limited
Tel: 01225 719204   Fax 01225 712187
E-mail circletime@jennymosley.co.uk

28a Gloucester Road
Trowbridge
Wiltshire BA14 0AA

Website www.circle-time.co.uk